THE 21ST CENTURY
COMMEMORATION
AND HISTORY OF
CRISPUS ATTUCKS DAY

THE 21ST CENTURY COMMEMORATION AND HISTORY OF CRISPUS ATTUCKS DAY

He Was The First to Defy, and The First to Die and His Name is Crispus Attucks!

Haroon A. Rashid and The Friends
of Crispus Attucks Association

The Pointe! Image Book Publishing
Boston MA

THE 21ST CENTURY
COMMEMORATION
AND HISTORY OF
CRISPUS ATTUCKS DAY

Published by:
The Pointe! Image Book Publishing
Boston MA
friendsofcrispusattucksboston@gmail.com

Haroon Rashid, Publisher / Editorial Director
Yvonne Rose/Quality Press.info, Book Packager
Cover image by The Friends of Crispus Attucks Association NFP

ALL RIGHTS RESERVED

No parts of this book may be reproduced or transmitted in any form or by any means electronic or mechanical, including photocopying, recording or any information storage and retrieved system without the written permission from the authors, except for the inclusion of brief quotations in review.

The publication is sold with the understanding that the Publisher is not engaged in rendering legal or other professional services. If legal advice or other expert assistance is required, the services of a competent professional person should be sought.

Copyright © 2021 by Haroon Rashid
Paperback ISBN #: 978-1-0879-7536-8
Hardcover ISBN #: 978-1-0879-0199-2
Ebook ISBN #: 978-1-0879-7538-2
Library of Congress Control Number: 2021916745

DEDICATION

FOCAA dedicate this book to a great American Legend and pioneer, Crispus Attucks, and to the many American Leaders and Associations that have followed in his footsteps, as patriots' heroes and she-roes, from the 18th to the 21st century that in their own ways have recognized Crispus Attucks and in some ways have aspired to leadership and equal human rights in America. We also dedicate this book as a new vision for the next generation of leaders, in 21st century America. The FOCAA contend that we as a people must respect the value and contributions of diversity, and inclusion from leaders such as Crispus Attucks, to President Barrack Obama, as true American history-makers. These are just two examples of many that represent leadership from the 18th to the 21st century African American diaspora, that are connected to the City of Boston. Others that we recognize are: Attucks *Father:* Prince Yonger, his *Mother:* Nany (Nancy) Attucks, *Sister:* Phoebe Attucks, *American statesman, political philosopher:* Samuel Adams, John Adams, Paul Revere, George Washington, William Cooper Nell, Charles Redmond, Lewis Hayden, and Joshua B. Smith, and the 54th Massachusetts Regiment of the United States Colored Troops, William Trotter, Wampanoag -Natick Praying Indians, Fredrick Douglas, *The June 19, 2021 federal holiday enactment:* Juneteenth Day, the African Renaissance Monument, also referred to as the Monument De La Renaissance Africaine: *Senegalese President:* Aboulaye Wade, Bingu wa Mutharika, the Malawian and African Union president, as well as the African presidents of Benin, Cape Verde, Republic of Congo, Ivory Coast, Gambia, Liberia, Mali, Mauritania, Zimbabwe, Ghana, South Africa, and Nigeria, Descendants of the Transatlantic African Slave Trade in America, The African Moors, Queen Charlotte of Great Britain, Duchess of Sussex

The 21st Century Commemoration and History of Crispus Attucks Day

Megan Markle, King of England, King George III, The Apostle John Elliot, the Boston Massacre Monument; Robert Kraus, sculptor, 1856 Legislator Anson Burlingame, Crispus Attucks Plaque Monument; Boston Equal Rights League; United State Senator Edward W. Brooke, State Senator William Owens, Deputy Mayor of Boston Clarence "Jeep" Jones, Irish American poet and civil rights activist John Boyle O'Reilly. The Black Revolutionary War Patriots Silver Dollar focuses on Crispus Attucks' Mint Director Philip N. Diehl, James Armistead, Crispus Attucks burial site at the Boston Granary Burying Ground, Prince Hall, George Middleton, the known member that was in the "Black-Bucks of America", Human-Rights-Abolitionist Harriet Tubman, Abolitionist Sojourner Truth, Human-Rights-Abolitionist Fredrick Douglas, Susan B. Anthony, Josephine St. Pierre Ruffin, Carter G. Woodson, and Dr. Martin Luther King, Melena Agnes Cass, Malcom X., Nelson Mandela the 1st Black President of the Republic of South Africa, President Barack Obama, The African American History Museum, The Revolutionary Spaces in Boston, The City of Boston, The Boston Public Catholic and Charter Schools, Boston Human Rights Commission, The Boston Youth Leadership Association.

ACKNOWLEDGMENTS

The FOCAA cannot thank enough all of the dedicated, brilliant and talented board members: Robert Redd - James Harris – Cynthia Strong - Rickie Thompson - Nathaniel Smith - Kelly Smith - Joe Pendarvis - Abdou Thiaw - Paul Goodnight - Azell Martin, and Associates: Darryl Smith - John Jones, the City of Boston Honorable Madam Mayor-Kim Janey, Nate Sheidley - Boston History Museum - Boston - Revolutionary Spaces, the Boston Human-Rights Commission Executive Director Evandro Carvalho, The Boston Youth Leadership Association, The African American History Museum, The Native American History Museum, Boston Mayor Martin Walsh, Boston Latin High School, Boston English High School, Boston City Councilor Andrea Campbell, Boston City Councilor Michelle Wu, Jackie Payne Thompson: Boston Equal Rights League, The Boston NAACP Association, The Honorable Madam Mayor of Framingham Yvonne Spicer, and the countless others.

If there is anyone or enactments that I might have missed in the list of persons and organizations in this book, I apologize; and please let me know so that we can make the adjustments.

The 21st Century Commemoration and History of Crispus Attucks Day

PREFACE

WHY WE WROTE THIS BOOK

The Friends of Crispus Attucks Association Inc. is a not-for-profit corporation that is dedicated to preserving the legacy of Crispus Attucks in the City of Boston and the State of Massachusetts. As we look at the 21st century information about Crispus Attucks, there are many people who know Attucks was the first adult casualty of the American Revolution and leader of the patriot group that rallied against the Redcoats on King Street in Boston. This event would later become known as the Boston Massacre. Crispus Attucks (c.1723 – March 5, 1770) was an African American sailor, thought to be the first leader killed, of the five men shot, in the historical Boston massacre. He is also widely referred to as the first American killed at the beginning of the American Revolution and the first martyr for the cause of American patriotism for Equal Human Rights. Many have given a history of Attucks that will tell you who he was and what he did, and how that caused him to be seen as the Boston Martyr and an American War Patriotic. But there has been no logical explanation for his reasoning of *why*, in knowing that he was then considered a runaway slave in the Boston area and yet he willingly sacrificed his freedom and ultimately his life at the historical Boston Massacre. Much has been written about Crispus Attucks' Native American heritage stemming from his mother. But little has been recorded about his West-African roots that he inherited from his father's side, and how his father was known as a Noble Prince in his homeland, but as a slave in America called Prince Yonger. A note of reference is that in the 1770's it was also well-known that globally Noble black men and women had the tendency to be referred to as Moors or Free Blacks. As you will see in our information about the timing of Attucks' final years, it is during that time the Queen Mother of Great Britain in England was Queen Charlotte, a black Moor. We believe this was a deliberate omission so that a critical portion of American history would forget about Attucks' personal heritage in the African Diaspora. In the 21st century, however, it is clear that Attucks certainly played a major role in his public activism to martyrdom in American history. As a result, the Friends of Crispus Attucks in Boston invite you to read a version of our research, in hopes that there will be greater transparency and understanding of the historical narrative of Boston's first "Revolutionary-War-Patriot" and Martyr Crispus Attucks. We believe this type of missing information is critical in the 21st century, especially during the era of a rise in racial diversity and inclusion for equal human rights in America.

That is why we wrote this book.

INTRODUCTION

HE WAS THE FIRST TO DEFY, THE FIRST TO DIE, AND HIS NAME IS CRISPUS ATTUCKS!

In America when you speak about iconic history makers at the beginning of America's advocacy for sovereign independence, there is one man in Boston's history that stands out as the First to Defy, The First to Die, and His Name Is Crispus Attucks! In this book the *Friends of Crispus Attucks Association* in Boston has assembled a historical timeline of information from the 16th to the 21st century that speaks about the experience of people from the African Diaspora during the historical inhumane Trans-Atlantic Slave-Trade business era. We will attempt to share some of this information on how, in spite of the historical disadvantages of chattel slavery and the inhumane treatments of systematic racism in America, history has documented Crispus Attucks as the one man in a critical moment of heroism; and that on March 5, 1770 he became forever referred to as the American Revolutionary War Patriot for Equal Human Rights.

In this book we start our collage of information with a colossal image of a 21-century statue tribute from a group of multicultural global leaderships, known as the African Renaissance Monument in Dakar Senegal. The statue monument gives a narrative of how the trilateral transaction of slavery from Africa through Europe to America, will lead to a direct connection to Crispus Attucks. The book gives further information about the history of the global slave trade and the mysterious lifestyle and interactions with the Free-Blacks, or the African Moors in Boston during the 1770's.

The 21st Century Commemoration and History of Crispus Attucks Day

This book is designed to give a more enlightened perspective about Crispus Attucks' link to a noble African heritage from his father and how having that knowledge influenced his eventual sacrifice for equal human rights. It is important to know that in the 21st century after America has elected its 1st African American President Barack Obama and the 1st African American woman as the Vice President Kamala Harris, the spirit of multicultural diversity and inclusion in leadership is now a new world order of reality, with its roots that can be equated to the true legacy of Crispus Attucks in America, which is, that of EQUAL HUMAN RIGHTS in leadership.

We share this information for the youth and future American leaders, with a reminder of the time that we all share as a collective body of diverse citizens for potential multicultural public leadership.

We trust that you will enjoy our research and information about a great American History-Maker: Crispus Attucks!

CONTENTS

Dedication v
Acknowledgments vii
Preface ix
Introduction xi
He Was the First to Defy, The First to Die,
And His Name Is Crispus Attucks! xi
Contents xiii

PART ONE: His Name Was Crispus Attucks 1

Chapter One: How Multicultural Global Leadership
Began in America 3

Chapter Two: The African Moors 21

Chapter Three: Queen Charlotte of Great Britain 27

Chapter Four: King of England, King George III 30

Chapter Five: Prince Yonger 34

Chapter Six: The Wampanoag –Natick Praying Indians ... 38

Chapter Seven: The Boston Massacre 45

Chapter Eight: Crispus Attucks Statue, Monuments
& Enactments in Boston 56

PART TWO: American Heroes that were inspired by The Honorable Crispus Attucks... 67

Chapter Nine: Prince Hall.. 69

Chapter Ten: Black Bucks 1775, American Revolutionary War, Black Soldiers 72

Chapter Eleven: Human Rights Abolitionist: Harriet Tubman 75

Chapter Twelve: Sojourner Truth... 79

Chapter Thirteen: Frederick Douglass... 81

Chapter Fourteen: The "Juneteenth" Freedom Day.......................... 93

Chapter Fifteen: Susan B. Anthony 110

Chapter Sixteen: William Cooper Nell... 112

Chapter Seventeen: William Monroe Trotter 115

Chapter Eighteen: Josephine St. Pierre Ruffin 117

Chapter Nineteen: Carter G. Woodson... 119

Chapter Twenty: Martin Luther King Jr... 121

Chapter Twenty-One: Senator Ed Brooks 123

Chapter Twenty-Two: Melnea Agnes Cass...................................... 125

Chapter Twenty-Three: Malcom X 128

Chapter Twenty-Four: South Africa President, Nelson Mandela... 130

Chapter Twenty-Five: President Barack Obama 132

About the Authors... 138

PART ONE

HIS NAME WAS CRISPUS ATTUCKS

The 21st Century Commemoration and History of Crispus Attucks Day

CHAPTER ONE

HOW MULTICULTURAL GLOBAL LEADERSHIP BEGAN IN AMERICA

The African Renaissance Monument

This is an important 21st century image of the African Renaissance Monument along with information that helps explain and makes the connection of the first Boston Martyr Crispus Attucks with the continent of Africa. Many have asked about the cultural and family roots of Crispus Attucks. For example, how did he and his family come to reside in the Commonwealth of Massachusetts? On the other hand, the African Renaissance Monument is referred to as the Monument De La Renaissance Africaine. It is a bronze statue perched on a hill in Dakar, Senegal. This image of a man, woman and child emerging from a volcano was inaugurated at a ceremony on April 3, 2010, featuring hundreds of drummers and dancers. The African Renaissance Monument stands erected against the West African skyline in Senegal.

In 2010 the unveiling marked Senegal's 50 years of independence. Senegalese President Aboulaye Wade has said he hopes the public monument will attract tourists to the West African country, and defended the public monument in writing, stating "this African who emerges from the volcano, facing the West ... symbolizes that Africa has freed itself from several centuries of imprisonment in the abyssal depths of ignorance, intolerance and racism, to retrieve its place on this land, which belongs to all races, in light, air and freedom."

"It's impossible to miss Senegal's new 160-foot (49 meters) African renaissance monument," wrote NPR reporter Ofeibea Quist-Arctan. Quote: "Perched high on a hill is the mighty Soviet-style bronze statue of a man, woman and child that overlooks the Atlantic Ocean."

It is important to note that the African Renaissance Monument dominates the capital city of Dakar. Furthermore, nineteen African heads of state attended the unveiling ceremony in Dakar. Notable public dignitaries included Bingu wa Mutharika, the Malawian and African Union president, as well as the African presidents of Benin, Cape Verde, Republic of Congo, Ivory Coast, Gambia, Liberia, Mali, Mauritania, Zimbabwe, South Africa and Nigeria.

Additionally, a delegation of 100 African Americans attended the ceremony, including Reverend Jesse Jackson and Senegalese American singer Akon. "It brings to life our common destiny," said President Wade at the unveiling ceremony, according to a Reuters report. "Africa has arrived in the 21st century standing tall and more ready than ever to take its destiny into its hands." The sculpture depicts a woman holding onto a man as he is holding a child pointing to a future and sacrifice that would be made; and eventually lead the way for all human life in North America. We contend that child is to be the Martyr of the Boston Massacre, Crispus Attucks.

THE HISTORY OF THE TRANS-ATLANTIC SLAVE TRADE

Let us dig into the history of the trans-Atlantic slave trade, that led to the immigrant slavery in New England and had a direct connection to Crispus Attucks' African heritage from his father Prince Yonger. History tells us that Prince Yonger was also a victim of the Trans-Atlantic slave trade. In accordance with historical records, there were eight principal areas that were used by Europeans to ship and buy slaves, during the Trans-Atlantic slave trade in the Western Hemisphere. It is important to know that the percent of enslaved people who were sold to the Europeans at that time varied throughout the slave trade era. Between 1650 and 1900, it has been estimated that

10.2 million enslaved Africans arrived in the Americas from the following regions in the following proportions:

- Senegambia (Senegal and the Gambia): 4.8%
- Upper Guinea (Guinea-Bissau, Guinea and Sierra Leone): 4.1%
- Windward Coast (Liberia and Ivory Coast): 1.8%
- Gold Coast (Ghana and east of Ivory Coast): 10.4%
- Right of Benin (Togo, Benin and Nigeria west of the Niger Delta): 20.2%
- Right of Biafra (Nigeria and east of Niger Delta Cameroon, Equatorial Guinea and Gabon): 14.6%
- West Central Africa (Republic of Congo, Democratic Republic of Congo and Angola): 39.4%
- Southeastern Africa (Mozambique and Madagascar): 4.7%

During the Trans-Atlantic slave trade the different ethnic groups that were brought to the Americas closely corresponded to the regions of heaviest activity in the slave trade. It is important to know that, as it has been recorded at that time, there was potentially an estimate of some 50 ethnic groups of slaves. Listed below are the ten most prominent ethnic groups recorded, according to slave documentations of that historical era.

1. The Kongo of the Democratic Republic of Congo and Angola
2. The Mandé of Upper Guinea
3. The Gbe speakers of Togo, Ghana, and Benin (Adja, Mina, Ewe, Fon)
4. The Akan of Ghana and Ivory Coast
5. The Wolof of Senegal and the Gambia

6. The Igbo of southeastern Nigeria
7. The Mbundu of Angola (includes both Ambundu and Ovimbundu)
8. The Yoruba of southwestern Nigeria
9. The Chamba of Cameroon
10. The Makua of Mozambique

The first steps toward an Atlantic slave trade made by Europeans were in the 1440s when Portuguese sailors landed in West Africa in search of gold, spices, and to get allies against the Muslims and the Ottoman Empire who dominated the then Mediterranean trade businesses. When the Portuguese landed on the coasts of Africa, they found societies engaged in a network of trade routes that carried a variety of goods back and forth across sub-Saharan Africa. Some of those goods included kola nuts, shea butter, salt, indigenous textiles, copper, iron and iron tools, and most importantly people for sale as slaves within West Africa. It has been heavily recorded that the new arrival of European slave traders in Africa also followed Muslim traders by some eight centuries. For as early as the seventh century, Muslims from North African and other areas of the Mediterranean world had established trade routes into Saharan and sub-Saharan Africa and acquired gold, pepper, ivory, dried meat, and hides, as well as slaves, which they then transported throughout North Africa, the Middle East and beyond.

The sub-Saharan African societies routinely discussed and participated in the slave trade business as either the enslaved or as slavers or brokers. While Europeans created the demand side for slaves, it was the African political and economic elites that did the primary work of capturing, and then transporting and selling Africans to European slave traders along the African coastal boarders. The European traders were vastly outnumbered by West Africans who controlled trade along the coast, they first had to negotiate with powerful African chiefs who often demanded a tribute and fair-trading terms. Only then could European traders be allowed to acquire African slaves. The most important and constantly asked question is, what was the reason, and why did the Africans participate in the slave trade?

Given its drain on the most productive adults from Africa's populations, the slave trade was also complex, especially at a time of African sovereignty and their Noble kingdoms. Furthermore, the violence and war sown by the slave trade greatly disrupted African societies. One answer is that the institution of slavery already existed in African societies. Slavery in Africa, however, was different from the kind of slavery that evolved in the European World, particularly in the English colonies. Many of those enslaved, and brought to the European countries and colonies, were the same people who had participated in local and long-distance trade. Unlike most of the European immigrants and or settlers that they encountered that were for the most part unskilled and illiterate, and ultimately depending upon their resources, they were skilled agriculturists. In other words, they were master artisans of textiles, bronze, gold, ivory sculpture, jewelry, and sacred objects. Some were also craftsmen of wooden tools, furniture, and architectural elements, as well as potters and blacksmiths. Others were skilled linguists in more than one African language and often one or more European languages as well. In some cases, they had developed trade languages that facilitated inter-group communication, even among African people whose language they did not know.

History shows upon research that one of the greatest ironies is that even though those who were brought to America, enslaved, and became part of one of the most heinous historical tragedies, these enslaved Africans in North America also became part of one of the greatest triumphs of human history. African people and their descendants helped to develop the modern Western world and created a new nation in the process that would lead to the spirit of human rights in America such as the legacy of Crispus Attucks. The Trans-Atlantic Slave Trade was a time of great struggle in Europe, from the ninth through the fifteenth centuries.

The European powers struggled with one another for territorial and commercial dominance of power. Case and point, there was a constant struggle between Western and Eastern Christendom and with Islam for religious and cultural dominance in Europe. The struggle for religious dominance resulted in North African Berbers, Mid-Eastern Arabs and other Muslim peoples from Morocco occupying the Iberian Peninsula for 700 years from 712 A.D. to 1492 A.D. During this time, while the Iberian powers sought to free themselves of Moorish occupation, England and France embarked on the Crusades to retake the Holy Land from Muslims, whom Christians called the "infidels". As the fifteenth century ended, Europeans embarked upon exploration of the New World and Africa in search of expanded territory, new goods, precious metals, and new markets. All these enterprises required manpower to explore, clear land, build colonies, mine precious metals, and provide the settlers with subsistence. In the New World, Europeans first tried to meet these needs by enslaving the American Indians and relying on European indentured laborers. Nevertheless, war, disease and famine among Native Americans and European settlers depleted the colonies' already limited labor force supply.

When both sources proved inadequate to meet the needs for labor, Europe then turned to Africa. The development of economies based on production of sugar, tobacco and eventually rice were contingent upon workers with attributes of material cultural knowledge, agricultural skills, and the physical capability to acclimate to the New World environment. The Africans that were first enslaved by the Spanish and Portuguese demonstrated that they were the people who overwhelmingly had the skills that could fulfill those requirements. In the sixteenth century, the Spanish conquistadores sailed to the Americas lured by the prospects of finding gold. They brought a few Africans as slaves with them. Early Spanish settlers soon were reporting that in mining operations the work of one African was equal to that of four to eight Indians. That promoted the idea of Africans as slave labor would be essential to the production of goods needed for the European colonization. There were several factors combined to give value to the Spanish demand for an African workforce.

- Native Americans died in large numbers from European diseases for which they had no immunity.

- At the same time, the Spanish clergy interceded to the Spanish Crown to protect exploitation of Indians in mining operations.

- The introduction of sugarcane as a cash crop was another factor motivating the Spanish to enslave Africans.

- To turn a profit, Spanish planters needed a large, controllable work force, they turned to Africa for Labor.

Once Portugal and Spain established the profitability of the African slave trade, other European nations entered the field. The English made an initial entry into the African slave trade in 1530 when William Hawkins, a merchant of Plymouth, visited the Guinea Coast and left with a few slaves.

Queen Elizabeth I rewarded to John Hawkins, a crest of a Negro's head and bust with its arms bound secured.

Three decades later Hawkins' son, John, set sail in 1564 for the Guinea Coast. Supported by Queen Elizabeth I, he commanded four armed ships and a force of one hundred and seventy men. Hawkins lost many of these men in fights with "Africans" on the Guinea coast in his attempts to secure Africans to enslave. Later through the actions of piracy he took 300 Africans from a Spanish vessels, making it profitable for him to head for the West Indies where he could sell them for money and trade them for provisions. Queen Elizabeth I, rewarded Hawkins for opening the slave trade for the English by knighting him and giving him a crest that showed a Negro's head and bust with arms bound secure.

How did Race become A Factor in The Slave Trade business: European participation in African enslavement can only be partially explained by economics? At the end of the medieval period, slavery was not widespread in Europe. It was mostly isolated in the southern fringes of the Mediterranean. Iberian Christians mostly enslaved Muslims, Jews, Gypsies, and Slavs who were "white" non-Christian eastern Europeans from whose name the word "slave" derives. When the transatlantic slave trade in Africans began in 1441, Europeans placed Africans in a new category. They deemed them natural slaves, a primitive, heathen people whose dark skin confirmed their God-ordained inferiority and subservience to Christian Europeans.

How the Curse of Ham in the Christian religion was used to Justify Black Slavery: The bible says that a curse of Ham occurs in the Book of Genesis, which states that a curse was imposed by Ham's father Noah. It occurs in the context of Noah's drunkenness and is provoked by a shameful act perpetrated by Noah's son Ham, who "saw the nakedness of his father" and allegedly did not cover his father's naked body, but instead he looked at his father and did nothing. However, it is written that Noah's younger son Shem, upon seeing his father's nakedness covered his body from shame. It further states that a penalty of the curse was then placed upon Ham's eldest Son among his Hamites descendants Canaan, who is the father of the (Canaanites), but not upon Shem and his descendants the Shemites, that instead was attributed favorability and with the blessings from God.

The story's original purpose may have been to justify the subjection of the Canaanite peoples to the Israelites, however somewhere in the later centuries, the narrative had then been interpreted by some Christians, Muslims, and Jews as an explanation for the black skin and a justification for slavery. To further the racial narrative of blacks in connection to Ham's son Canaan, a Persian historian named Muhammad ibn Jarir al-Tabari recounted a tradition that the wife of Canaan was named Arsal, a daughter of Batawil son of Tiaras, and that she bore him the "Blacks, Nubians, Fezzan, Zanj, Zaghawah, and all peoples of the Sudan". Likewise, Abd al Hakam tells that "Canaan is the father of the Sudan (Sub Saharan Africans) and the Abyssinians".

Europeans thus created an emergent understanding of "race" and racial difference based on divine heritage from their participation in the transatlantic slave trade and a system of racism codified in law and policy and driven by a desire for wealth and profit. The first transnational, institutional endorsement of African slavery occurred in 1452 when Pope Nichols V granted King Alphonso V of Portugal the right to reduce all the non-Christians in West Africa to perpetual slavery. Note: (Queen Charlotte, of Great Britain was a "Black Moor", and a direct descendant of the Portuguese King Alfonso III).

By the second half of the fifteenth century, the term "Negro" had become essentially synonymous with "slave" across the Iberian Peninsula and had literally come to represent a race of people, most often associated with black Africans, who were considered to be inferior. In the seventeenth century, Spanish colonizers created a Sistema de castas, or caste system, that ranked the status and power of peoples based on their "purity of blood." Spanish elites born in Spain sat at the top of this racial classification system while African slaves occupied the bottom. Skin color thus correlated with status and power. Race-based ideas of European superiority and religious beliefs in the need to Christianize "heathen" peoples contributed to a culture in which enslavement of Africans could be rationalized and justified.

Western and African historians agree that war captives, condemned criminals, debtors, aliens, famine victims, and political dissidents were subject to enslavement within West African societies. They also agree that during the period of the transatlantic slave trade, internal wars, crop failure, drought, famine, political instability, small-scale raiding, taxation, and judicial or religious punishment produced many enslaved people within African states, nations, and principalities.

There is a consensus among scholars that the capture and sale of Africans for enslavement was primarily carried out by the Africans themselves, especially the coastal kings and the elders, and that few Europeans ever actually marched inland and captured slaves themselves. African wars were the most important source of enslavement. It is important to recognize, however, that there did not exist a common shared "African" identity among African peoples during the early stages of the transatlantic slave trade along the coast of West Africa. Consequently, when traders from West African kingdoms sold men, women, and children to European slave traders, most would have thought they were selling outsiders, rather than fellow Africans, from their societies and kingdoms of people who spoke different languages, who were prisoners of war or criminals, debtors, and dissidents.

Just as there were wars between Europeans over the right to slave catchment areas and points of disembarkation, there were increasing numbers of wars between African principalities as the slave trade progressed. Whatever the ostensible causes for these wars, they resulted in prisoners of war that supplied slave factories at Goree and Bance Islands, Elmina, Cape Coast Castle, and James Forts and at Fernando Po along the West and West Central African coast.

The fighting between African societies followed a pattern. Wars weakened the centralized African governments and undermined the authority of associations, societies, and the elders who exercised social control in societies with decentralized political forms. The winners and losers in wars both experienced the loss of people from niches in lineages, secret societies, associations, guilds, and other networks that maintained social order. Conflict brought about loss of population and seriously compromised indigenous production of material goods, cash crops and subsistence crops.

While the slave trade often enriched the West African kingdoms that controlled the trade along the coast, it had a devastating impact on the societies. African societies lost kinship networks, agricultural laborers, and production. The loss of people meant the loss of indigenous artisans and craftsmen, along with the knowledge of textile production, weaving and dying, metallurgy and metalwork, carving, basket making, potting skills, architectural, and agricultural techniques upon which their societies depended. Africa's loss was the New World's gain. These were the same material cultural expertise and skills that Africans brought to the New World along with their physical labor and ability to acclimate to environmental conditions that made them indispensable in the development of the Western Hemisphere.

The Portuguese dominated the first 130 years of the transatlantic African slave trade. After 1651 they fell into second position behind the British who became the primary carriers of Africans to the New World, a position they continued to maintain until the end of the trade in the early nineteenth century. Based on data concerning 86 percent of all slaving vessels leaving for the New World, historians estimate that the British, including British colonials, and the Portuguese account for seven out of ten transatlantic slaving voyages and carried nearly three quarters of all people embarking from Africa destined for slavery.

France joined the traffic of slaves in 1624, Holland and Denmark soon followed. The Dutch wrested control of the transatlantic slave trade from the Portuguese in the 1630s, but by the 1640s they faced increasing competition from French and British traders. England fought two wars with the Dutch in the 17th century to gain supremacy in the transatlantic slave trade. Three special English companies were formed, including the "Royal African Company", to operate in the sale of slaves. They were given the exclusive rights to trade between the Gold Coast and the British colonies in America.

As the 17th century ended in 1698, English merchants' protests led to the English crown extending the right to trade in slaves more generally. Colonists in New England immediately began to engage in slave trafficking. Vessels left Boston, Massachusetts and Newport, Rhode Island laden with rum that was exchanged for people in Africa consequently enslaved in North American and Caribbean colonies.

Beginning with the Spanish demand for slave labor, a demand that continued and expanded in the other colonies and the United States even after the abolition of the slave trade in 1807, the Transatlantic Slave Trade brought between 9.6 to 11 million Africans to the New World. Greater numbers of people were sold into slavery from some regions as compared to other regions. Some European nations transported more Africans than others and some regions in the New World received more Africans from certain regions than others. Again, the British and Portuguese account for seven out of every ten transatlantic slaving voyages and carried nearly three quarters of all people embarking from Africa destined for slavery.

Individual merchants as well as pirates found it profitable to beat the Dutch monopoly and transport slaves directly from West Africa to the West Indies. The English came up with further innovations in the organization of trading corporations. The Dutch trading companies had displaced the monarchs of Spain, but they too tried to maintain a monopoly on this trade. By contrast, the English opened their trading companies to all merchants. This had the effect of discouraging piracy. Given a stake in the overall profits, British interlopers found it more advantageous to join this new company than to fight it. In 1750, the old Royal African Company was dissolved and replaced by a new corporation called the "Company of Merchants Trading in West Africa".

By 1713, the Dutch were exhausted and many of their holdings on the coast of Africa and in the Indian Ocean had fallen to their enemies. England established itself on the southern coast of Guinea in West Africa around the modern nations of Ghana and Nigeria, while the French won the northern coasts around Senegal and Gambia. In 1713, the British and the French won concessions from Spain to supply slaves to the Spanish colonies in America. Between 1713 and 1763, France and England fought for the possession of trading routes and for colonies in America and India. The British, with their superior business acumen, triumphed. In 1757, the Battle of Plassey near Calcutta sealed not only the fate of the French effort in India but of India itself.

As the British gained dominance of the oceans, the Atlantic slave trade gathered momentum. English and French immigration to the American colonies increased, and with it the cultivation of sugarcane and cotton. Demand for slaves outpaced their supply. Whereas the total number of slaves shipped from West Africa to Portugal between 1441 and 1500 was about 30,000, the number between 1700 and 1800 was close to seven million. The total number displaced from all of Africa between 1441 and 1840 exceeded ten million. Untold numbers died at sea. The sick were cast overboard; women abused.

In the 19th century, when the British navy imposed a search and impound policy toward slave ships, entire "cargoes" were thrown overboard to prevent the ships from being impounded. Many more millions were killed in the tribal wars that were fought in Africa to capture the slaves. When all these numbers are added up, a conservative figure for the total casualties of the Atlantic slave trade would be fifteen million. (To bring these numbers into perspective, the total population of England around the year 1600 was estimated to be at six million). More than 60 percent of the captives were from West Africa, a region under Islamic influence for centuries. The others came from Angola in West Africa and Mozambique in East Africa, which became the primary sources for slaves sent to Brazil.

It may be deduced that up to twenty percent of all slaves transported to the Americas were Muslim. Africa was denied the energy of its young men and its young women. Instead, they became a line item in the enormous capital-accumulation taking place in Europe and the Americas. The oppressed and the oppressor both suffered. The casualty was the slave, the slave catcher and the slave owner. Christian and Muslim together paid the price.

The slave trade broke down African social structures. Until the 15th century, East Africa was a part of the iron culture linking the lands of the Indian Ocean. West Africa was linked to the Mediterranean by trade routes across the Sahara. The slave trade interrupted the natural evolution of African culture. The captured Africans were not the savages and cannibals that they were portrayed to be. They were masons, carpenters, jewelers, and scholars like the people of Asia and Europe. Centralized empires existed in Mali, Songhay, the Congo and Rhodesia. No such centralized authority could emerge after the European intervention.

From the Muslim perspective, the slave trade destroyed trading patterns in the Maghrib, enslaved many Muslims both in West and East Africa, marginalized West Asia by circumventing its trade routes, and ultimately led to its colonization. The importance of the Atlantic slave trade decreased as the industrial revolution gathered momentum. Unit labor costs became much lower for machine labor than they were for human labor. The overhead for the transportation of slaves was high and profitability of the trade decreased. The slave trading nations realized that there were more profits to be made by colonization and by peaceful trade than by the slave trade.

Towards the end of the 18th century, a minority opinion in England and in the United States spoke up against this inhuman trade. They were helped in their cause by the Industrial Revolution. The British Parliament abolished the slave trade in England in 1772, coincidently just two years after the Boston Massacre. Denmark passed similar legislation in 1803. The United States abolished it in 1808, and Holland in 1818. Even as the curtain fell on the Atlantic slave trade, a scramble ensued for colonies and raw materials required for the industrial infrastructure of Europe. Illegal traffic persisted until 1840. To stop it, Britain entered mutual search treaties with other maritime nations of the Atlantic to search America-bound ships for human cargo. This effort was only partially successful, so the British navy undertook to patrol, search and confiscate any ship with contraband slave cargo.

It was not until 1850 that the Atlantic slave trade finally came to an end. Abraham Lincoln abolished slavery in America in 1863. The survival and prosperity of Africans in the New World is a testament to the triumph of human endurance and of the indomitable spirit of humankind. It is of special importance to note that during that time in the colonial history, that there were men of African descent who were classified as freemen in the Boston area. These men were basically seamen who exercised their Sovereign Human rights, traveling from seaport to seaport to earn a living for themselves and their families. They were referred to as "African Moors!

CHAPTER TWO
THE AFRICAN MOORS

Moorish Chief, 1878 painting: by Eduard Charlemont

The 21st Century Commemoration and History of Crispus Attucks Day

Who were the African Moors, and how did they have so much prestige and influence in Europe and the new world in the Americas?

This is a list of bullet point reasons that will give some insight to that question, as well as some brief information about the African Moors:

- The Spanish occupation by the African Moors began in 711 A.D. when an African army, under their leader Tariq ibn-Ziyad, crossed the Strait of Gibraltar from northern Africa and invaded the Iberian Peninsula 'Andalusia' (Spain under the Visigoths).

- The Moors, who ruled Spain for 800 years, introduced new scientific techniques to Europe, such as an astrolabe, a device for measuring the position of the stars and planets; and Scientific progress in Astronomy, Chemistry, Physics, Mathematics, Geography, and Philosophy flourished throughout Moorish Spain.

- Basil Davidson, one of the most noted historians recognized and declared that there were no lands at that time (the eighth century) "more admired by its neighbors, or more comfortable to live in, than a rich African civilization which took shape in Spain".

- At its height, Cordova, the heart of Moorish territory in Spain, was the most modern city in Europe. The streets were well-paved, with raised sidewalks for pedestrians. During the night, ten miles of streets were well illuminated by lamps. (This was hundreds of years before there was a paved street in Paris or a streetlamp in London.) Cordova had 900 public baths; it is written that a poor Moor would go without bread rather than soap!

- The Great Mosque of Córdoba (La Mesquita) is still one of the architectural wonders of the world in spite of later Spanish disfigurements. Its low scarlet and gold roof, supported by 1,000 columns of marble, jasper, and porphyry was lit by thousands of brass and silver lamps which burned perfumed oil.

- Education was universal in Moorish Spain, available to all, while in Christian Europe ninety-nine percent of the population were illiterate, and even kings could neither read nor write. At that time, Europe had only two universities, the Moors had seventeen great universities! These were in Almeria, Cordova, Granada, Juen, Malaga, Seville, and Toledo.

- Over 4,000 Arabic words and Arabic-derived phrases have been absorbed into the Spanish language. Words beginning with "al," for example, are derived from Arabic. Arabic words such as algebra, alcohol, chemistry, nadir, alkaline, and cipher entered the language. Even words such as checkmate, influenza, typhoon, orange, and cable can be traced back to Arabic origins.

- The Moors introduced paper to Europe and Arabic numerals, which replaced the clumsy Roman system.

- The African Moors introduced many new crops including the orange, lemon, peach, apricot, fig, sugar cane, dates, ginger and pomegranate as well as saffron, cotton, silk, and rice, which remain some of Spain's main products today.

- It was through Africa that the new knowledge of China, India, and Arabia reached Europe. The Moors brought the Compass from China into Europe.

It is quite common that when the topic of the Moorish influence in Europe is being discussed, one of the first questions that arise is, what race were they? The term "Moor can be found throughout literature, art, and history books, it does not actually describe a specific ethnicity or race. Instead, the concept of Moors has been used to describe alternatively the reign of Muslims in Spain, or sometimes Europeans of African descent. The word Moor is derived from the Latin word "Maurus," the term was originally used to describe the Berbers, and other people from the ancient Roman province of Mauretania, in what is now North Africa. Over time, it was increasingly applied to the African Muslims living in Europe. During the beginning of the Renaissance, the terms "Moor" and "blackamoor" were also used to describe any person with the dark skin of prestige and value. In accordance to the Oxford English Dictionary, as early as the Middle Ages, "Moors were commonly viewed as being mostly black or very swarthy, and hence the word Moor is often used to describe negro," and some historians have written that "the original Moors, like the original Egyptians, were also black Africans."

Noted that the 16th century English playwright William Shakespeare used the word Moor as a synonym for African, and would also use African and Moor interchangeably, and many Arab writers further referred to the black identity of the Moors. It is written that the powerful Moorish Emperor Yusuf ben-Tach fin is described by an Arab chronicler as a "brown man with wooly hair." History records that Black soldiers, specifically identified as Moors, were actively recruited by Rome, and served in Britain, France, Switzerland, Austria, Hungary, Poland, and Romania. The Black Moor, "St. Maurice", which was a patron saint of medieval Europe, was only one of many black soldiers and officers under the employ of the Roman Empire. Spanish rulers have tried to expunge this era from the historical record for generations, but more recent archaeology and scholarship have shed fresh light on the African Moors who flourished in Al-Andalus for more than 700 years, from 711 A.D. until 1492. History will show that it was the Moorish advances in mathematics, astronomy, art, and agriculture helped propel Europe out of the Dark Ages and into the Renaissance.

Universal Education during the 10th and 11th Centuries

The African Moors brought critical learnings to Spain, that over centuries would spread throughout the rest of Europe. The intellectual talents and achievements of the Moors in Spain at that time had a lasting effect.

In the 10th and 11th centuries, Moorish Spain could boast of more than 70 public libraries, including one in Cordova that housed hundreds of thousands of manuscripts, while in Europe they were nonexistent. The Universities in Paris and Oxford were established after visits by scholars to Moorish Spain. It became this system of education that was taken to Europe by the Moors, that created the European Renaissance and brought the continent out of the dark ages and 1,000 years of intellectual and technological gloom of the Middle Age era.

It is important to note that during the time of Attucks, Boston was under the international sovereignty, the United Kingdom of Britain, and under the royalty of King George and Queen Charlotte. What is of further importance, and that makes the connection to the African Moors at that time was that Queen Charlotte was an African Moor herself. That factor alone was one of the many reasons that the sea merchants that would travel into the British colony of Boston had so much liberty and prestige among the colonists, as well as the military forces of Great Britain. But it is easy to imagine that many of the local colonists had mixed feelings about the Black Moors because of the chattel permanent-slavery conditions for black slaves, versus the white indentured- slaves, that had the benefit of a timeline for the opportunities of freedom. Unlike the Black slaves in the same region, even though at that time, the Queen Mother of Great Brittan and the Boston colony was herself, a powerful Royal Black woman.

CHAPTER THREE
QUEEN CHARLOTTE OF GREAT BRITAIN

Queen Sophie Charlotte of Mecklenburg-Strelitz

So, who exactly was Queen Charlotte? Here are a few things to know about the British royal: Charlotte of Mecklenburg-Strelitz, originally named Sophie Charlotte was born: on May 19, 1744, she died: November 17, 1818, at the age of (74). Queen Charlotte also held the titles of Electress of Hanover and Queen Consort of Hanover. Mecklenburg-Strelitz was a minute north of German dukedom in the Holy Roman Empire. Queen Charlotte was the youngest daughter of the royal Princess Elizabeth Albertine Saxe-Hildburghausen, and Duke Charles Louis Frederick of Mecklenburg-Strelitz, otherwise known as Prince of Mirow. Queen Charlotte is a descendant of a black branch of the Portuguese royal family; more specifically, King Alfonso III and his concubine, Madraana, a Black Moor. Queen Charlotte was chosen to be George III's bride. It is recorded that at age 17, she traveled from Germany to England to marry King George III, and it's believed that King George III's mother had chosen her to marry her son. Queen Charlotte had 15 children: but just 13 survived childhood, after Queen Charlotte married George III in 1761, she gave birth to 15 children. Being almost constantly pregnant weighed on her. Quote: "I don't think a prisoner could wish more ardently for his liberty than I wish to be rid of my burden and see the end of my campaign. I would be happy if I knew this was the last time," she wrote in 1780 about her pregnancy with her 14th child, Prince Alfred, according to Janice Hadlow's. *"The Strangest Family: The Private Lives of George III, Queen Charlotte, and the Hanoverians.*

Prince Alfred only lived for two years. He became ill after receiving an inoculation against the smallpox virus and died in 1782; soon after, Prince Octavius, who was 19 months Prince Alfred's senior, also died of smallpox in 1783. It is important to note that during the Boston historical enactment in 1770, Queen Charlette was 26 years old some 9 years after becoming the Queen of the United Kingdom. That undoubtedly lead to the complect perception of race and Royal Nobility as it related to the classification and character of the so-called Free-man, Blackamoor, and soon after the beginning of the Black Masonic fraternity in 1775, for either a black or white man during that important time in the American history. Footnote: These facts make today's Queen Elizabeth II, Prince Charles, Prince William, and Harry technically of mixed race, many historians have tried to cast doubt on the nature of Queen Charlotte's heritage. But her personal physician has noted her "true mulatto face" and in the public a report was released, before Queen Elizabeth II's coronation in 1953 acknowledging the monarchy's African heritage.

In this picture, the one on the left is Queen Charlotte of Great Britain during the time of 1770 Boston Massacre, and on the right is the Duchess of Sussex Megan Markle in 2021, who is a black woman; however history shows that she is not the first "Black Woman" to marry into the British Royal Family!

(quote): Africans don't beg for royalty. We know we are the originals and we have been there before anyone else. They just hide it, but we remember, and we will teach it to our children. - *"Michael Imhotep"*

CHAPTER FOUR
KING OF ENGLAND, KING GEORGE III

King George III

King George III (George William Frederick; born, 4 June 1738 – died 29 January 1820) was King of Great Britain and Ireland from 25 October 1760 until the union of the two kingdoms on January 1, 1801. Then after which he was King of Great Britain, and the United Kingdom and Ireland until his death in 1820. He was concurrently Duke and Prince-elector of Brunswick-Lüneburg ("Hanover") in the Holy Roman Empire before becoming King of Hanover on October the 12, 1814. He was a monarch of the House of Hanover, but unlike his two predecessors, he was born in Great Britain, spoke English as his first language, and he had never visited Hanover. George's life and reign, which were longer than those of any of his predecessors, were marked by a series of military conflicts involving his kingdoms, much of the rest of Europe, and places further afield in Africa, the Americas, and Asia. Early in his reign, Great Britain defeated France in the "Seven Years' War", becoming the dominant European power in North America and India. However, many of great Britain's American colonies were lost soon after the war for the American independence, and further wars against revolutionary Napoleonic France from 1793 concluded in the defeat of Napoleon at the Battle of Waterloo in 1815.

In the later part of King George's life, he had recurrent and eventually permanent mental illness. Although it has since been suggested that he had suffered from bipolar disorder or the blood disease porphyria, the cause of his illness remains unknown. After a final relapse in 1810, a regency was established. Then his eldest son, Prince George, of Wales, ruled as the Prince Regent until his father's death, when he succeeded as George IV. Historical analysis of George III's life has gone through a "kaleidoscope of changing views" that have depended heavily on the prejudices of his biographers and the sources available to them.

King George was born in London at Norfolk House in St James's Square. He was the grandson of King George II, and the eldest son of Frederick, Prince of Wales, and Augusta of Saxe-Gotha. As he was born two months prematurely and thought unlikely to survive, he was baptized the same day by Thomas Secker, who was both the Rector of St James's and Bishop of Oxford. One month later, he was publicly baptized at Norfolk House, again by Secker. His godparents were King Frederick I of Sweden and his uncle Frederick III, Duke of Saxe-Gotha. Prince George grew into a healthy, reserved and shy child. The family moved to Leicester Square, where George and his younger brother Prince Edward, Duke of York and Albany, were educated together by private tutors. King George and Queen Charlotte's marriage: In 1759, George fell in love with Lady Sarah Lennox, sister of Charles Lennox, 3rd Duke of Richmond, but Lord Bute advised him against the match and George abandoned his thoughts of marriage.

He wrote, "I am born for the "happiness or misery" of a great nation, and consequently I must often act contrary to my passions. Nevertheless, attempts by the King to marry George to Princess Sophie Caroline of Brunswick-Wolfenbüttel were resisted by him and his mother. The following year, at the age of 22, George III succeeded to the throne when his grandfather, George II, died suddenly on 25 October 1760, just two weeks before his 77th birthday. The search for a suitable wife intensified. On the 8th of September 1761 in the Chapel Royal, St James's Palace, the King married Princess Charlotte of Mecklenburg-Strelitz, whom he met on their wedding day. Two weeks later on 22 September, both were crowned at Westminster Abbey. History reveals that King George remarkably never took a mistress (in contrast with his grandfather and his sons), and the couple enjoyed a happy marriage until his mental illness struck. They had 15 children, nine sons and six daughters. In 1762, George purchased Buckingham House, on the site now referred to as the Buckingham Palace, for use as a family retreat for the Royals. His other residences were Kew Palace and Windsor Castle. St James's Palace was retained for official use. He did not travel extensively and spent his entire life in southern England. That leads us to Crispus Attucks and his father "Prince" Yonger, whose legacy was that of he is being the decedent of an African Moor-like legacy.

CHAPTER FIVE

PRINCE YONGER

Prince Yonger with his wife Nanny Peter-Attucks and son Crispus Attucks

Crispus Attucks (c.1723 – March 5, 1770) was an American stevedore (sea merchant) of African and Native American descent, and he is widely regarded as the first person killed in the Boston Massacre and thus the first American killed in the American Revolution. Historians disagree on whether he was a free man or an escaped slave, but most agree that he was of Natick and African descent. Two major sources of eyewitness testimony about the Boston Massacre published in 1770 did not refer to him as "black" not as a "Negro"; it appears that Bostonians viewed him as being of mixed ethnicity. According to a contemporaneous account in the *Pennsylvania Gazette*, he was a "Mulattoe man, named Crispus Attucks, who was born in Framingham. In the history of Crispus Attucks, it reveals a known major factor that Crispus Attucks as a young youth who was born into slavery, became curious and uncomfortable regarding his understanding of him being classified as a slave and in knowing that the Black Moors who traveled in and out of Boston were called Black Freemen. It is safe to say that knowledge or information is considered a major reason that Attucks became ambitious to advocate for his own personal freedom and social "Equal Human Rights".

Crispus Attucks was one of two children, and his father "Prince" Yonger, as he was called, was from West Africa. When Prince Yonger was a child, he was captured by tribal enemies, and then after his capture he was sold into the "Transatlantic Slave Traders". They then brought him to America, by way of the West Indies Islands, where he became transformed and then labeled as a $3/5^{th}$ (human-chattel property slave). He eventually was brought to Boston after being purchased to serve for his British slave master in the town of Framingham near the Boston settlement. It is believed that because Prince Yonger was raised before being captured, and then sold into slavery as a young Royal figure, that had an effect of respect from other slaves that knew of Prince's legacy, and because he was taught skills of an agriculturist as a child in his homeland by his father, who was a Tribal Chief in Africa, he was considered of great value to his slave master in America, Colonel Joseph Buckminster, and he was then converted into a house slave and field slave supervisor.

There is little known of exactly what tribal nation or republic that Prince came from through the Transatlantic Slave Trade, but there is some speculative evidence which suggests that Crispus Attucks' father Prince Yonger, may have been an African-born slave, from Nigeria of the Yoruba people, or from Senegal of the Wolof people, in West Africa. It has been said by elders that Crispus Attucks and his sister Phebe were told that by their father one day, after their begging him to explain to them about his African heritage and history. Prince Yonger explained to them for the first time that his father was a West African chief, of a large African empire that was divided into large sections of territories and peoples. Within each section was governed and led by a leader that was called Fari; and as a Fari, he ruled over many chiefs known as Nois. Each of these Nois were in control of large cites. It was also a given fact at that time that all Nois would have large armies, which were necessary to fight off enemies that would try to take their property and possessions.

Prince's father had seven sons and each of them was given the opportunity to do the thing that they loved the most under his kingdom. Prince, loved the idea of growing things and he mastered the art at a young age, so much so that his father put him in charge of a large body of tribesmen for agriculture leadership. It was at one of those critical tribal war incidents of Chief Yonger that brought about a tribal war during which Prince's father was killed, and Prince as a young boy was sold into slavery which made him a "Noble" Prince, in his father's native land in Africa. But sadly, in America he was just another slave owned by a white political leader and plantation owner named Colonel Joseph Buckminster.

Prince Yonger became unbelievably valuable and trustworthy as an agriculturist on the plantation of Colonel Buckminster, and he was given what was considered good treatment compared to the many other field slaves that had a lesser sophisticated character and skill set experience than "Prince" Yonger. It is important to know that Colonel Buckminster and his wife were devoted Christians that were following in the tradition of the famous British Christian religious leader John Eliot. It was with that in mind that the Buckminster's worked to convert Prince and they were instrumental in helping him meet and marry his wife, Nancy Attucks (Nanny-Peter-Attucks). They had a traditional Christian wedding, and they were happy to be together.

Crispus Attucks mother's name is Nanny Peter-Attucks; she was a Natick Native American Indian from the Wampanoag tribe that was called the Praying Indians in New England. It is important to note that it was the custom of the Indigenous people that the women, when giving birth to a child, would pass down the women's families last name to their children, instead of the men's last names. That is why Crispus and his sister Phebe's last names are their mother's family name (Attucks), and not their father's (Yonger), as it is now written in the history of Crispus Attucks.

CHAPTER SIX
THE WAMPANOAG –NATICK PRAYING INDIANS

Nancy Attucks: (Nanny-Peter-Attucks) meaning- "Small Dear"

Nanny or Nancy Attucks had a dark and troubled history about her people, like her husband, that she always hesitated to talk about because of the pain she had in the memory of what had happened to her family and people by the white invaders that migrated into their land; and how they stripped them of both their land and their sovereign human rights.

*The Apostle John Elliot: John Eliot's "Indian Bible"
by Elijah M Haines (1888)*

John Elliot (1604 – May 21, 1690) was a Puritan missionary to the American Indians, whom some called "the Apostle to the Indians" and the founder of Roxbury Latin School in the Massachusetts Bay Colony in the year 1645.

Nancy Attucks told her children about a white Minister named John Elliot, who was called by his followers the Apostle Elliot. She said that his only interest in Native Americans was to convert them and to teach them about his interpretation of God and the religion of Christianity, as he saw it. She said that in the year of 1650 he persuaded and converted a large band of Indians to start a Christian religious settlement in the town of Natick, Massachusetts. He also persuaded the British government to let the Native Americans have control of their own land in exchange for their other lands in the western part of the territory; essentially the First People in Massachusetts were giving up their rights to their own Sovereign lands. Then after the Native American settled in Natick, they were thereafter known as the Natick Praying Indians.

History says that all the First People in the area did not agree with the land grab takeover and new culture that was forced on them by the new immigrants, so they resisted. It did not take long when a war had begun and at the end of the war all the Native American men in the region were either killed or exported as slaves into a foreign land that they did not have any familiarity or knowledge of in Great Britain, the United Kingdom. Just the women and children were left to fend for themselves and they were given a colonized title of being called the Praying Indians. Crispus' mother, Nanny Attucks, had the experience in not only losing her family, but she also was stripped of her culture and forced to look outside of her own people for a mate as all the Praying Indian women were forced to do in her time. Nanny was introduced to Prince by Mrs. Buckminster and her husband Colonel Buckminster and they both where baptized and married as Christians in the new Christian religion.

The Wampanoag –Natick Praying Indians

*Crispus Attucks learning about freedom
from field slaves. Library of Congress*

In Crispus' time, a field slave was the most rebellious of the slaves. Even though Crispus Attucks' father was treated well, and his master was considered by Crispus as a kind person, the influence of the field slaves made Crispus know he did not and would not be a willing or volunteer slave. As much as he loved his mother and father, he vowed that he would not be subjugated to following in their footsteps, as a house slave or servant, so he eventually became a runaway slave. Little is known about the early years of Attucks. He was born a slave in the (then) colony of Massachusetts. His father, Prince Yonger, was African and his mother Nanny Peter-Attucks, was an American Indian and she was a possible descendant of John Peter-Attucks, who was a member of the Natick Indian tribes. John Attucks was an immensely powerful and respected leader in his tribal nation that was executed for treason by the British in 1676 during the King Philip War.

The word "Attucks" in the Natick language means "Small Deer. It was also known that, at that time, the field slaves on the plantation were often running away for freedom, and as Crispus and his sister Phebe became more aware of these acts, they questioned their mother and father about the notion of freedom. Prince Yonger and Nancy Attucks became concerned about their enquiry since one of the field slaves who was friendly and close to the children had just lost her husband who ran away seeking freedom. It is said that Crispus became sympathetic to the field slaves reasoning for running away for freedom and of his growing ambition of becoming a seaman like the African Moors that traveled back and forth to Boston. Prince and Nanny became concerned that Crispus might be influenced enough by the local field slaves that were planning such escapes. Prince had a talk with his slave master Colonel Buckminster, who he knew cared about Crispus, to see if he could talk to Crispus and persuade him not to run away; and that he would be offered his freedom at the right time.

But after Colonel Buckminster talked to Crispus he was convinced that Crispus would eventually run away in search of his desire to be free. In Colonel Buckminster's discussion with Crispus, he discovered that Crispus really wanted to be a sea merchant or to work in the harbor, so Colonel Buckminster talked to a friend and fellow slaveowner that had a horse farm and small ships that he would use sometime to travel near Boston. Colonel Buckminster then sold Crispus to Mr. William Brown and told Crispus and his parents that even though he would be leaving his parents he will be near enough to make visits and he will be near the boat and harbors that he always wanted to experience.

In 1750, young Attucks, as a slave of William Brown in Framingham, became a successful horse and cattle trader who did business with

The Wampanoag – Natick Praying Indians

white men. He used the money he made to try to buy his freedom from his owner, Mr. William Brown, but he repeatedly refused his offer. Attucks then ran away, and he was never caught; and nothing was known of him for nearly 20 years before he resurfaced again. Historians record that he escaped to Nantucket, MA, and sailed as a harpooner on a whaling ship.

Soon after running away, he found work as a sea whaler. After learning this, he distinguished himself as a master in his craft. He then went on to be considered and to consider himself as a Free Black man. Even though on the plantation that his father worked, and he grew up on, he was still considered a runaway slave. It is recorded that at age 27 there was a reward for him, as a runaway slave named "Crispas" that was published on October 2, 1750, for an offering of 10 pounds for his return. It read: ("Ran-away from his Master William Browne of Framingham, on the 30th of September, that he was seen last, he is a Mulatto Fellow, about 27 years of age, named Crispus, six feet, two inches high, with short curl's Hair"). Spelling standards back in the day were more relaxed, and historians have assumed "Crispus" and "Crispas" were the same name.

Attucks became a sailor for whaling vessels, and records show that he often traveled as a deception under an alias name of "Michael Johnson" in certain ports of entry. As a sailor, Attucks was under constant threat of conscription into the British military. Most sailors did not like the compulsorily to enroll for service in the armed forces, and Attucks did not either. Nor did he enjoy the company of British soldiers. The Friday before the massacre in 1770, Attucks and his companions chased a British soldier out of a tavern and got in a scuffle with three other British soldiers, as a result. One of the most important factors of Crispus Attucks' life was, one day as Crispus Attucks was visiting Boston from a sea journey he became angry over the way the British military were interacting with a young white man; a scuffle between large gatherings of colonial citizens began. Because of that, he took a position and acted as their leader, to take a stand against the military. Things got out of control and he consequently was shot and killed. That act of courage motivated the citizens to protest the ending of British colonization, that lead to the saying, "no taxation without representation "and beginning of the war between British and American Patriots, that led to independence from England and British control.

That blind act of courage comes from men or women when they feel they are free to demand for their Equal Human Rights; this action will impulsively give them respect from most people. So, when you think of the American Revolution, what words come to mind? Many people think of the British soldiers and their red coats, the Boston Tea Party, the Founding Fathers, and the Constitution. Many also have the impression of the American colonies' efforts by whites to gain independence, and that the American Revolution and all the important things that happened in it were entirely the result of people of European descent. We think this because of how we have been taught American history in schools. When we look at the actual history, though, we see a different picture that would surprise a lot of people, for example the first school in America, the Roxbury Latin School, in the Massachusetts Bay Colony in the year 1645, was a missionary school for Native Americans.

CHAPTER SEVEN

THE BOSTON MASSACRE

This is a 19th-century lithograph image: it is a variation of the famous engraving for the Boston Massacre: by Paul Revere.

The lithograph was produced soon before the American Civil War and long after the Boston Massacre event depicted, in this image it emphasizes Crispus Attucks as a Black man, who had become a symbol for the abolitionists. (John Bufford after William L. Champneys, ca. 1856)

What We Know about Crispus Attucks' Early Life as a martyr and patriot: Despite the lack of clarity, Attucks became an icon of the anti-slavery movement in the mid-19th century. In the 1850s, as the abolitionist movement gained momentum in Boston, supporters lauded Attucks as an African American who played a heroic role in the history of the United States. Historians disagree on whether Crispus Attucks was a free man or an escaped slave, but most agree that he was a man of Wampanoag and African descent. Two major sources of eyewitness testimony about the Boston Massacre, both published in 1770, did not refer to Attucks as "black" nor as a "Negro", instead it did appear that Bostonians of European descent viewed him as being of a mixed ethnicity.

According to a contemporary account in the *Pennsylvania Gazette* (Philadelphia), he was a "Mulatto man, or commonly known as a Black Moor: named Crispus Attucks, who was born in Framingham. It is safe to say that, at that time, the European white settlers could have made a connection of value with the mixed ethnic appearance of Crispus with that of Queen Charlotte of England, especially because of his mixed heritage. Attucks' story is also significant for Native Americans, as well as people of the African diasporic descent.

The Boston Massacre: In the fall of 1768, British soldiers were sent to Boston in an attempt to control growing colonial unrest, which had led to a series of attacks on the local officials following the introduction of the Stamp Act and the subsequent Townshend Acts. The Radical Whigs as they were called, was a group of British political commentators that were associated with the British Whig faction, and they were at the forefront of the radical movement, that had coordinated waterfront mobs against the authorities. The presence of British troops, instead of reducing tensions, only served to further inflame them.

1769, Crispus Attucks returned to Boston during a time of great tension, because of King George III of England's actions to rule the American colonies, without regards for their rights. The colonists were angry and felt that they were being taken advantage of by their mother country. Crispus witnessed, one day, a colonial leader named James Otis in an argument with British army officers, when one of the officers struck Mr. Otis over his head with a sword that the people said caused him to have a permanent mental illness. Crispus witnessed that incident that caused major unrest between the people of Boston and the British soldiers before he left to go on another sea journey.

Upon his return on February 22, 1770 trouble between the people and the solders had again gotten more radical and intense. A protest occurred outside a British customs house, and a man named Ebenezer Richardson, who worked there, tried to break up the protest. Instead of stopping the crowd he instead lured their protest to his house. To ward off the protesters, who were throwing rocks, Richardson fired a musket shot into the crowd from his window. He wounded a teenager and murdered an 11-year-old child. Crispus was there and he silently observed this tragedy and attended the boy's funeral, and he was struck by the young boy's death as the boy's death was treated as an act of martyr. Attucks also attended the trial in court when Mr. Richardson was found innocent and set free. He, like many of the colonists felt that he should have been punished. It is no surprise, that the history of Crispus' life and his personal survival from slavery made him feel more of the need to advocate, whenever necessary, for the causes of human rights, and freedom for himself and anyone else in the Boston colony during that time in his life.

After the trial, Crispus was seen mingling through the crowds in the streets and squares. He would ask, "What do you think about the way the King's solders are treating you?" Their answer was that "We hate it". He felt a mission to use the incident to address the organizing for freedom and human rights; he then became a leader of the colonists. Those feelings created a riff that was triggered by the King's Tax demands. The great Boston colonial leader, Samuel Adams, who was representing the colonists tried to settle the tax issues with the English parliament before then, and the King ignored his letter for support. Someone asked "What can we do? They said that they came to America to be free, but King George will not grant the freedom that other Englishmen enjoy in Great Britain." It was at this point when they asked Crispus Attucks who was standing on a platform listening behind the Old State House.

Crispus replied that laws have been passed to interfere with trade, to help make English merchants make greater profits that we must pay for at our expense. He then suggested that they disperse and return on a new day and things might be cleared up then. The crowd began to disperse in groups. Crispus, before leaving himself, went over to the Captain that was there with a large group of soldiers who had said to him to stop arousing an angry mob, and said, "You think I am arousing the people! Then what do you think that you are doing? You and your solders are the ones that are stirring things up. "He further said, "The sight of you is just as maddening as a red flag is to a bull." He then turned his back and strode away leaving the Captain angerly staring at him.

On March 5, 1770, after dusk, a crowd of about twenty-eight colonists confronted a sentry who had chastised a boy for complaining that an officer did not pay a barber's bill. Both towns' people and a company of British soldiers of the 29th Regiment gathered. Crispus heard the alarms and came to see what was happening. After observing the situation and the apparent fear in the faces of the colonists, he determined that they would need more men to help if there was a battle. He told a few of the leaders in the crowd that he would be back after he goes down to the harbor and brings back some help with him. He further said that when you refuse to pay King George's taxes, he sends his solders. Crispus made the comment that was heard by gathering solders nearby. "It is not fair that King George would send his solders to enforce his laws." A solder then shouted, "Who says so?" As the crowed stared at him, he then clutched his musket as though he was ready to shoot. Crispus responded "I say so!" He further commented that it takes a coward to mistreat people with guns in your hands. He further said, "Put down the guns and we will show you how to fight fairly. It was at that moment that Crispus was perceived by the solders and the colonists as a leader among the colonists. The crowd in return cried out "Yes, Yes!"

That is when the solder and his comrades started to retreat to the barracks. The colonists threw snowballs and debris at the soldiers. The solders fell back and sent for Captain Preston, who then quickly came to the square with additional solders. The war-like positioning of the solders, frightened the crowd as they began looking for Crispus, who was now their leader. Then, just as the crowd was beginning to get nervous and afraid, they asked, "Where is Crispus?" Suddenly a large group of 50 to 60 men, mostly sailors, including Crispus Attucks, approached the Old State House armed with clubs. It then got quiet and a few of the solders fled; but Captain Preston and his guards remained, as they looked for Crispus. It is important to know that a key moment in the history of Crispus Attucks, and his short life after, began when the British commanding officer, Captain Thomas Preston, came rushing forward, shouting "Stop this confusion!" He then singled out and pointed at Crispus. He then demanded that Crispus would come down from that platform and to stop arousing the people.

The 21st Century Commemoration and History of Crispus Attucks Day

Crispus Attucks and sailor companions confronting the British: Painting by George Gaadt

Crispus then demanded that they, the British guards, put down their weapons and fight like men. Captain Preston then pointed at Crispus, and a shot was fired. They said that a soldier was struck with a piece of wood, and claimed it was done by Attucks. Other witnesses stated that Attucks was "leaning upon a stick" when the soldiers opened fire. Five colonists were killed and six were wounded. Attucks took two ricocheted bullets in the chest and was believed to be the first to die. County coroner's Robert Pierpoint and Thomas Crafts Jr. conducted an autopsy on Attucks. Crispus Attucks' body was then carried to Faneuil Hall by the orders of Samuel Adams, where it lay in state until

Thursday, March 8, 1770 when he and the other victims were buried together in the same gravesite in Boston's Granary Burying Ground. He had lived for approximately 47 years before his death.

Reaction to the trial: Notably, John Adams was assigned to successfully defend most of the accused British soldiers against a charge of murder. Two were found guilty of manslaughter. Faced with the prospect of hanging, the soldiers pleaded *"benefit of clergy"*. They were instead branded on their thumbs. (Benefit of Clergy Law) (Latin: *privilege clerical*) was originally a provision by which clergymen could claim that they were outside the jurisdiction of the secular courts and be tried instead in an ecclesiastical court under canon law. Various reforms limited the scope of this legal arrangement to prevent its abuse, including branding of a thumb upon a first use, to limit the number of further invocations for some.

In John Adams arguments, he called the crowd a motley rabble of saucy boys, Negros and Mulattos, Irish Teague's and outlandish Jack Tars. In particular, he charged Attucks with having "undertaken to be the hero of that night," and with having precipitated a conflict by his so-called "mad behavior. Two years later United States Founding Father, Samuel Adams, that was a cousin of John Adams, named the event the "Boston Massacre," and helped ensure that the event would not be forgotten.

The Boston artist Henry Pelham the (half-brother of the celebrated portrait painter John Singleton Copley) created an image of the event. Paul Revere made a copy from which prints were made and distributed. You will discover that some copies of the print show a dark-skinned man with chest wounds, presumably representing Crispus Attucks. Other copies of the print show no difference in the skin tones of the victims. The five who were killed were buried as heroes in the Granary Burying Ground, which also contains the graves of Samuel Adams, John Hancock, and other notable figures. While custom of the period discouraged the burial of black people and white people together, such a practice was not completely unknown. Prince Hall, for example, was interred in the Copp's Hill Burying Ground in December 1807 at the North End of Boston 39.

What Led to the Boston Massacre?

It was unfair British Tax Laws, that until the Boston massacre, the British controlled the trade vessels of the American colonies through what was called the Navigation Acts, and at that time they also were known to have taxed the colonies without any representation, and the colonists did not like that. So, it became a popular thing that they would often boycott any businesses whose owners were loyal to the British. Then, after the massacre, they would later routinely say. "Remember, Remember, the Fifth of March!"

This became the beginning of the tribute honoring of Crispus Attucks, and despite the then laws and customs of regulating and segregating the burial of blacks, Crispus Attucks was buried in the Park Street Cemetery with the other honored men that died from the massacre: Samuel Gray-Ropemaker, James Caldwell-Shipmate, Samuel Maverick-Ivory Turner, and Patrick Carr-Leatherworker. After the massacre, for years, the colonists in Boston would observe March 5th as a the day of remmeberance. Several years later on March the 5th during the fortification of Boston colonists in the preparation for a battle agnist the British, General George Washington, as a way of rallying the solders said, "Remember, it is the fifth of March and avenge the death of your bretheren".

President George Washington

General George Washington, lifted a prohibition against blacks in Virginia who enlisted in the Continental Army, and then opened the ranks to free black men. The signing of the Declaration of Independence had not yet happened, for years this event was the most important day of remembrance for the colonists during the Revolutionary error. Hundreds of colored soldiers fought in the Revolutionary War.

For several reasons, however, comparatively little is known about the valuable service they rendered. As a rule, they fought side by side with white soldiers, and not in separate companies. The credit for the deeds of valor they performed, therefore, has gone to the military units to which they belonged, rather than to the race with which they were identified. However, if you had happened to be in Boston on the 5th of March 1770 walking down King Street (now known as State Street) you would have witnessed the incident to which George Washington referred. You would have seen a crowd of colonists who were excited and angry led by one who was darker in complexion than the others. You would have heard these men challenge, with great spirit, some British soldiers standing on guard. You would have seen these soldiers fire into the menacing crowd and kill the ringleader; then later you would have seen three of his comrades fall. The first victim of this clash between the colonies and Great Britain was Crispus Attucks, a colored man.

The signing of the Declaration of Independence had not happened yet, so for years this event was the most important day of remembrance for the colonists during the Revolutionary War. John Adams, a Founding Father who served as the second President of the United States, later wrote in hindsight that the Boston Massacre served as the "foundation of American independence" from British rule. Attucks, and his role also became a symbol against slavery to American abolitionists. In the mid-1800s, Thomas Sims, a fugitive slave from Georgia, was recaptured and dragged back into slavery in public, over the same street on which Attucks had died.

In May 1856 Legislator Anson Burlingame gave a speech about Sims a few months later in October in Boston. He said: The conquering of our New England prejudices in favor of liberty 'does not pay.' It 'does not pay,' I submit to play our fellow-citizens under practical martial law; to beat the drum in our streets; to clothe our temples of justice in chains, to creep along, by the light of the morning star, over the ground wet with the blood of Crispus Attucks, the noble colored man, who fell on King street before the muskets of Tyranny, away in the dawn of our Revolution, a man made in the image of God was led off to slavery, over the same spot where Hancock stood, and (ATTUCKS) fell where the Negro blood of (CRISPUS ATTUCKS) stained the ground over that spot, Boston authorities carried a citizen of Massachusetts to Alexandria as a slave. Where the disgusting rites of sacrificing a human being, to slavery were lately performed, the spot which was first moistened with American blood in resisting slavery, and among the first victims was a colored person.

CHAPTER EIGHT
CRISPUS ATTUCKS STATUE, MONUMENTS & ENACTMENTS IN BOSTON

Boston Massacre monument; Erected 1888 Robert Kraus, sculptor

The story of Crispus Attucks was embraced and elevated by abolitionists in the 1850s and his memory became a focal point for African American calls for citizenship, inclusion, and equality. In 1851, Black leaders - William Cooper Nell, Charles Redmond, Lewis Hayden, and Joshua B. Smith - petitioned the Massachusetts legislature for a monument in honor of Crispus Attucks. Black abolitionists inaugurated March 5th as "Crispus Attucks Day" in 1858.

Later, during the Civil War, Lewis Hayden would become a recruiter for the 54th Massachusetts Regiment of the United States Colored Troops, and Joshua Smith would play a critical role in persuading state officials to commission a memorial to Robert Gould Shaw and the Massachusetts 54th Regiment on Boston Common. The granite and bronze monument to the Boston Massacre was finally erected on the Boston Common, in collaboration with the Commonwealth of Massachusetts. Crispus Attucks has remained a symbol of African American struggle for freedom and equality, a Black hero, and a founding father of America. Attucks, immortalized as "the first to defy, the first to die," has been lauded as a true martyr, "the first to pour out his blood as a precious libation on the altar of a people's rights."

Inscription: (Sculpture, proper right:) HENRY BONNARD CO/NEW YORK 1888 (Sculpture, proper left:) ROBERT KRAUS FECIT/BOSTON 1888 (On bronze plaque, along the top:) FROM THAT MOMENT/WE MAY DATE/THE SEVERANCE OF/THE BRITISH EMPIRE. /DANIEL WEBSTER/ON THAT NIGHT/THE FOUNDATION OF/AMERICAN INDEPENDENCE/WAS LAID. /JOHN ADAMS (On bronze plaque, bottom right): Robert Kraus/Cast by the Henri Bonnard Bronze Co. 1889 On upper front of obelisk: CRISPUS ATTUCKS/SAMUEL MAVERICK/JAMES CALDWELL /SAMUEL GRAY/PATRICK CARR

The 21st Century Commemoration and History of Crispus Attucks Day

On lower front of obelisk reads: MARCH 5, 1770 - On lower rear of obelisk reads, ERECTED IN 1888, BY THE COMMONWEALTH OF MASSACHUSETTS IN HONOR OF THOSE WHO FELL AT THE BOSTON MASSACRE.

Description: The monument consists of an allegorical female figure representing the Spirit of the Revolution standing atop a granite base in front of a tall granite obelisk adorned with a band of thirteen stars around the top. The female figure is loosely draped and holds a furled American flag in her proper left hand. Her proper right arm is raised and in her proper right hand she holds a broken piece of chain. Beneath her proper right foot is a broken British crown. An eagle ready to take flight is perched by her proper left foot. On the base, beneath the female figure, is a bronze relief plaque depicting the Boston Massacre. It shows five men, *"CRISPUS ATTUCKS, SAMUEL MAVERICK, JAMES CALDWELL, SAMUEL GRAY, and PATRICK CARR"*, slain by the British soldiers in front of the Massachusetts State House. The hand of one victim and the foot of another, project from the surface of the relief. The hand is brightly polished by visitors who think they are shaking the hand of "Crispus Attucks."

THE CRISPUS ATTUCKS PLAQUE MONUMENT

Crispus Attucks Plaque monument Dedicated to the City of Boston by the Boston Equal Rights League in 1976.

The City of Boston held a ceremony in honor of Crispus Attucks, whom many considered an African American patriot and the first martyr of the American Revolution. The event began with a parade which proceeded past the Old Granary Burying Ground, where Attucks lies buried with the other victims of the Massacre, to Faneuil Hall. An estimated 450 people heard remarks by Edward W. Brooke, the first African American to be popularly elected to the United States Senate, and William Owens, Massachusetts' first African American State Senator. Clarence "Jeep" Jones, the first African American Deputy Mayor of Boston, presided over the ceremony. At the Old State House, The Equal Rights League dedicated a commemorative plaque to honor Crispus Attucks, which the Bostonian Society has in its collection today.

October 17, 1976: The year 1976 marked the two-hundredth anniversary of the ratification of the Declaration of Independence and the height of the bicentennial era. For marginalized peoples, especially African Americans, this was a fraught and confusing time. Some people questioned why African Americans should support the bicentennial at all, given the civil rights abuses they continued to suffer. By the mid-1970s, the city of Boston was still in the throes of conflict over racial desegregation with its implementation of busing desegregation from 1974 to 1988, which involved the transportation and exchange of students between black and white public schools. During the bicentennial period, white antibusing demonstrations tapped into public memory of the American Revolution, both intentionally and unintentionally.

In 1975, four hundred ROAR (Restore Our Alienated Rights) protestors picketed a Boston Massacre reenactment and dramatically fell to the ground when British soldier reenactors fired their guns. The following year, antibusing demonstrators infamously invited another comparison to the Boston Massacre when they attacked African

American lawyer Ted Landsmark. In a June 1976 editorial entitled "The Bicentennial Blues," *Ebony* writers marveled that this had taken place "within sight and sound of Faneuil Hall," near the site where Attucks had died. When Senator Brooke gave his *"1976 Crispus Attucks Day"* addresses at Faneuil Hall, he rightly observed: "Here and now in this room, you and I are still fighting for freedom…more than 200 years later." Brooke condemned the "white and black, separate and unequal" split in American society and American schools, and Senator Owens affirmed Attucks' reputation as a martyr who "gave his life" for all the people of Boston.

The Equal Rights League commemorative plaque features an excerpt from the poem, "Crispus Attucks," by Irish American poet and civil rights activist John Boyle O'Reilly. O'Reilly wrote the poem in 1887 or 1888 after the Massachusetts General Court announced its decision to erect a monument to the Boston Massacre in Boston Common.

At the dedication ceremony for the monument, which also came to be known as the "Attucks Memorial," a clergyman from New Bedford, MA, read O'Reilly's poem aloud in Faneuil Hall. Although O'Reilly's poem predated Boston's desegregation crisis by nearly a century, and is older still today, it remains painfully relevant.

Frustrated by the shortcomings of American freedom, O'Reilly wonders:

From "Crispus Attucks"

> And now, is the tree to blossom?
>
> Is the bowl of agony filled?
>
> Shall the price be paid, and the honor said, and the word of outrage stilled?

And we who have toiled for freedom's law, have sought for freedoms soul?

Have we learned at last that human right is not a part, but the whole?

That nothing is told while the clinging sin remains part unconfessed?

That the health of the nation is periled if one man be oppressed?

By: John Boyle O'Reilly, 1888.

A SILVER COIN IN HONOR OF CRISPUS ATTUCKS

In 1998 on the 275th anniversary of Crispus Attucks birth, the US Mint issued

Washington, D.C.: As the nation celebrates Black History Month, the Silver Dollar honoring the first Black Revolutionary War Patriot, and the first American to give his life in the Revolutionary War, is now available from the U.S. Mint.

"The Black Revolutionary War Patriots Silver Dollar focuses on Crispus Attucks' sacrifice and the commitment of all Black American Patriots," said Mint Director Philip N. Diehl. "It is particularly fitting that we recall their contribution during Black History Month, giving Americans the opportunity to learn about the role that Black Patriots played in our revolutionary struggle." Dozens of black Virginians fought and died with their white compatriots at Valley Forge and the 1st Rhode Island Regiment was composed entirely of 250 black soldiers. When the English General Cornwallis surrendered at Yorktown, he was shocked to find, at the side of General Lafayette, a black patriot named James Armistead. Cornwallis had believed that this master spy, a double agent, was working for the British. Altogether some 5,000 black patriots fought for freedom — although for many of them, only their descendants would be free. According to law, the U.S. Mint is authorized to produce up to 500,000 silver dollars to commemorate Black Revolutionary Patriots and the 275th anniversary of the birth of Crispus Attucks.

A portion of the proceeds from sales of the coins will support the construction of the Black Patriots Memorial on the National Mall in Washington, D.C. near the Lincoln Memorial and the Vietnam Veterans Memorial. The obverse of the silver dollar, designed by Mint Sculptor/Engraver John Mercanti, is a portrait of Crispus Attucks, the first patriot killed in the infamous Boston Massacre in 1770, the event that many historians believe triggered the Revolutionary War. The reverse design, by Ed Dwight, depicting a Black Patriot family, is also the design of the sculpture for the Black Patriots' Memorial, honoring not only the black soldiers who fought for freedom, but also the families who supported them. Dwight, the first African American to be trained as an astronaut, has created more than 55 monuments and memorials to honor notable African Americans, and his art appears in private collections, major museums and at the Smithsonian Institution.

Of special interest is the Black Patriot's Young Collector's Edition, the latest in the Mint's popular series. Limited to only 20,000 sets, it includes the Uncirculated Silver Dollar in an entertaining, informative package. In addition, the Mint is offering the Black Patriots Coin–and–Stamp Set, featuring the Proof Silver Dollar and four stamps honoring African American patriots who made significant contributions to our nation: abolitionist Frederick Douglas, inventor Benjamin Banneker, soldier Salem Poor, and Underground Railroad conductor Harriet Tubman.

One of the few men of color that have been given a US Mint issued silver coin in his honor. Crispus Attucks continues to be honored by the American public. In 1998, to commemorate the 275th anniversary of his birth, the US Mint issued a silver coin in honor of Attucks. Many schools, children's centers, foundations and museums are named after him representing the struggle and heroism of a black man searching for freedom.

CRISPUS ATTUCKS AT BOSTON GRANARY BURYING GROUND

Crispus Attucks and the five other martyrs who were killed: The grave is buried next to the man considered as United States' Founding Father, Samuel Adams, in the Boston Granary Burying Ground.

On March 8, 1770, the five who were killed were buried as heroes in the Granary Burying Ground, which also contains the graves of Samuel Adams, John Hancock, and other notable figures. While custom of the period discouraged the burial of black people and white people together, such a practice was not completely unknown. Prince Hall, for example, was interred in Copp's Hill Burying Ground in the North End of Boston 39.

The Granary Burial Ground is Boston's third oldest cemetery and was founded in 1660 when space at the King's Chapel Burial Ground was insufficient to meet the needs of a growing Boston population. The Granary Burial Ground is located on Tremont and Park Streets near Park Street Church. It was originally part of the Boston Common and was known as the South Burial Ground. In 1737 adjacent lots, which included the granary building and a house of corrections, were redeveloped into public buildings and private housing. The South Burial Ground took the name of Granary Burial Ground.

Many notable citizens are buried in the Granary: Declaration of Independence signers - John Hancock, Robert Treat Paine and Samuel Adams, and patriots - Paul Revere and James Otis. The parents of Benjamin Franklin and important politicians, literary authors and artists rest in this cemetery. It is believed that more than 5,000 bodies are buried at the Granary. There are 2,300 headstones, most families have one headstone.

PART TWO

AMERICAN HEROES THAT WERE INSPIRED BY THE HONORABLE CRISPUS ATTUCKS

The 21st Century Commemoration and History of Crispus Attucks Day

CHAPTER NINE
PRINCE HALL

1775: Prince Hall.

Hall was a freemason and a visionary. He recognized Attucks and the others who sacrificed their lives for the cause of freedom, and he became motivated to organize and advocate for the black freeman human rights!

Prince Hall grew up in Lexington, MA, the birthplace of the American Revolution and the place where Paul Revere rode through the town, saying, "The British are coming. The British are coming." Furthermore, he talked about how these men loved their country and should not forget their homeland." Nor should they let others forget, as well. Prince Hall became interested in the Masonic fraternity because Freemasonry was founded upon ideals of liberty, equality and peace.

Prior to the American Revolutionary War, Prince Hall and fourteen other free black men petitioned for admittance to the all-white Boston, St. John's Masonic Lodge, and they were turned down. Having been rejected by the Boston colonial Freemasonry, Prince Hall and 15 others sought and were initiated into the Masonry by members of Lodge No. 441 of the Grand Lodge of Ireland on March 6, 1775. The Lodge was attached to British forces that were stationed in Boston. Hall and other freedmen founded the African Lodge No. 1 and he was named the Grand Master. The Black Masons had limited power; they could meet as a lodge, take part in the Masonic procession on St. John's Day, and bury their dead with Masonic rites but they could not confer Masonic degrees or perform any other essential functions of a fully operating Lodge.

Being unable to create a charter, they applied to the Grand Lodge of England. It was Prince Henry, the Duke of Cumberland, and Strathearn, who was the sixth child and fourth son of Frederick, the Prince of Wales, and Princess Augusta of Saxe-Gotha, and a younger brother of King George III, that was given the authority, and he issued a charter for the African Lodge No. 1 that was renamed the African Lodge No. 459 September 29, 1784.

The lodge became the country's first African Masonic lodge. Due to the African Lodge's popularity and Prince Hall's leadership, the Grand Lodge of England made Hall a Provincial Grand Master on January 27, 1791. His responsibilities included reporting on the condition of lodges in the Boston area to the Grand Lodge of England. Six years later, on March 22, 1797 Prince Hall organized a lodge in Philadelphia, that was called the African Lodge #459, under Prince Hall's Charter. They later received their own charter. On June 25, 1797 he organized the African Lodge known as the Hiram Lodge #3 in Providence, Rhode Island.

CHAPTER TEN

BLACK BUCKS 1775, AMERICAN REVOLUTIONARY WAR, BLACK SOLDIERS

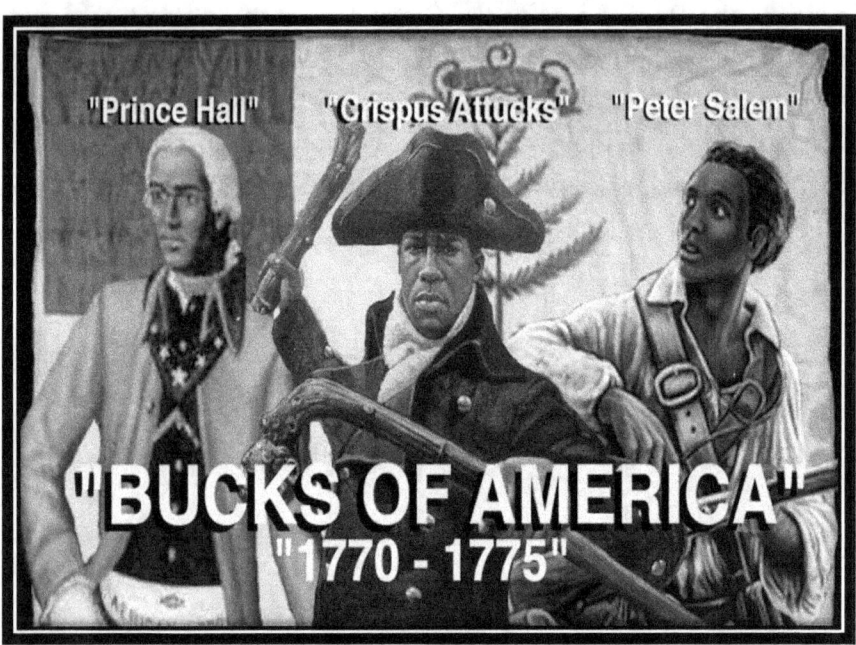

When the American Revolutionary War began in 1775, black soldiers, both slaves and freemen served with white soldiers in integrated militia units in the New England colonies. Later that year, these New England militia units became the nucleus of the newly created Continental Army, the national army of the colonies. The inclusion of black soldiers in the army was controversial.

By the end of 1775, the Continental Congress and the army's Commander-in-Chief, George Washington, decided to stop enlisting black soldiers. Washington soon reversed this decision, however, both because of manpower shortages and because the British had offered freedom to slaves who would escape from Patriot masters to join the British. Washington permitted free blacks to enlist in the Continental Army. White owners could enroll their slaves, as substitute forces, for their own service. On the local level, states made independent decisions about the enlistment of African Americans. Massachusetts continued to accept black soldiers in its integrated militia units.

However, on the local level, the states made independent decisions about the enlistment of African Americans. Massachusetts continued to accept black soldiers in its integrated militia units. It was also one of several northern states to create a segregated unit of black soldiers.

Blacks and abolitionists generally disapproved of the creation of segregated units, preferring integrated units. George Middleton was one member of the black Bucks of America. William Cooper Nell was said to be a member, and that he had claimed that he had attained the rank of a colonel while he had served. Middleton is one of the only known member of the "Bucks of America" to be known by name. It is highly believed that other members of his unit may also have been members of the Boston Prince Hall Freemasonry Lodge. History has recorded that Crispus Attucks' patriotism, represented the beginning of some 5,000 African American soldiers that is known to have fought for America's independence.

Bucks of America medallion is an engraved, oval, silver, planchet, with the letters "MW", on the bottom, thirteen stars, for the 13 United States, above a leaping buck, and a shield, with three, fleur de lis flowers, the crest, of the last French, royal family, the Bourbons, as a symbol of the Franco-American war alliance, made in honor and recognition of the All Black Patriot militia company.

CHAPTER ELEVEN

HUMAN RIGHTS ABOLITIONIST: HARRIET TUBMAN

Harriet Tubman was born Araminta Ross, 1822 – March 10, 1913.

The first twenty-five years of her life was spent as a slave on a Maryland plantation. She was a revolutionist and leader for the Underground Railroad. She had the courage of a commander and strategy of a general. She was called Black Moses because of her success in guiding her people out of the land and conditions of slavery.

After making her own escape, Tubman successfully made thirteen trips back and forth with a network of sympathizers and supporters to propel four hundred slaves to freedom. She did that with a $12, 000 Reward for her capture. Tubman was also called the "black shadow".

Much like in the spirit of Crispus Attucks she was well known in New England and Canada as one of the first African American leaders advocating for equal rights in the women's feminist movement. In 1850, Harriet Tubman was an abolitionist from Maryland, who took part in the Underground Railroad that led former slaves to Canada through Boston, along Columbus Avenue in the South End area.

Tubman knew Attucks' history and believed that all slaves should be free. In the early 1800s the movement continued in America with both blacks and whites fighting to abolish the institution of slavery, which continued until the Civil War. Many free African Americans joined the ranks of soldiers, nurses and cooks who fought for a country free of slavery, including Harriet Tubman who guided thousands of slaves to freedom and nursed soldiers and slaves to health during the Civil War.

Harriet Tubman's Suffragist Activism: In her later years, Tubman worked to promote the cause of the women's suffrage movement. It is written that a white woman once asked Tubman whether she believed women ought to have the right to vote, and she replied, "Yes, I suffered enough to believe it." She, soon after, began attending suffragist organizational meetings and was soon working alongside women such as Susan B. Anthony.

Tubman traveled to Boston, New York, and Washington, D.C. to speak out in favor of women's voting rights. She described her actions during and after the Civil War and used the sacrifices of countless women throughout modern history as evidence of women's equality to men. When the National Federation of Afro-American Women was founded in 1896, Tubman was the keynote speaker at its first meeting. This wave of activism kindled a new wave of admiration for Tubman among the press in the United States. A publication called The

Woman's Era launched a series of articles on "Eminent Women" with a profile of Tubman.

An 1897 suffragist newspaper reported a series of receptions in Boston honoring Tubman and her lifetime of service to the nation. She was an American abolitionist, humanitarian, and an armed scout and spy for the United States Army during the American Civil War. Born into slavery, Tubman escaped and subsequently made some thirteen missions to rescue approximately seventy enslaved families and friends, using the network of antislavery activists and safe houses known as the Underground Railroad. She later helped abolitionist John Brown recruit men for his raid on Harpers Ferry, and in the post-war era was an active participant in the struggle for women's suffrage.

Born a slave in Dorchester County, Maryland, Tubman was beaten and whipped as a child, by her various masters. Early in life, she suffered a traumatic head wound when an irate slave-owner threw a heavy metal weight, intending to hit another slave, but hit her instead. The injury caused dizziness, pain, and spells of hypersomnia, which occurred throughout her life.

Tubman was a devout Christian and experienced strange visions and vivid dreams, which she ascribed to premonitions from God. In 1849, Tubman escaped to Philadelphia, then immediately returned to Maryland to rescue her family. Slowly, one group at a time, she brought relatives with her out of the state, and eventually guided dozens of other slaves to freedom. Traveling by night and in extreme secrecy, Tubman (or "Moses", as she was called) "never lost a passenger". After the Fugitive Slave Act of 1850 was passed, she helped guide fugitives farther north into British North America, and helped newly freed slaves find work.

When the Civil War began, Tubman worked for the Union Army, first as a cook and nurse, and then as an armed scout and spy. The first woman to lead an armed expedition in the war, she guided the raid at Combahee Ferry, which liberated more than 700 slaves.

After the war, she retired to the family home on property she had purchased in 1859 in Auburn, New York, where she cared for her aging parents. She was active in the women's suffrage movement until illness overtook her and she had to be admitted to a home for elderly African Americans that she had helped to establish years earlier.

After she died in 1913, Harriet Tubman became an icon of American courage and freedom. On April 20, 2016, the U.S. Treasury Department announced a plan for Tubman to replace Andrew Jackson as the portrait gracing the $20 bill.

CHAPTER TWELVE
SOJOURNER TRUTH

1850s: Sojourner Truth was born into slavery as Isabella Bomfree.

In 1826 she escaped slavery to freedom with her infant daughter. in 1826. She had a spiritual vision and she pronounced that the Spirit called on her to preach the truth, thus adopting the name Sojourner Truth. She is most famously known for her speech, "Ain't I a Woman?"

Sojourner Truth challenged prevailing notions of gender, racial inferiority, and inequality. She supported herself as a journalist through sales of the *"Narrative"* and other mementos to the reform-minded audiences. Sojourner, while living in New York, had been in company and association as a journalist with newspaper owner and social activist Frederick Douglass.

During that time Douglass was a great advocate for the advocacy of America's 1st Patriot and Martyr for equal human rights, Crispus Attucks. After coming to Boston from New York, Sojourner was further encouraged by her knowledge of the Crispus Attucks legacy of equal-human-rights for all people in the Boston area. As a true powerhouse, she advocated for human rights for the rest of her life until she passed away in 1890.

CHAPTER THIRTEEN
FREDERICK DOUGLASS

1852: Fredrick Douglass, on February 5th published his newspaper, "The North Star", in Rochester New York.

The 21st Century Commemoration and History of Crispus Attucks Day

It reported: "On the 5th of March 1851, a petition was presented to the Massachusetts Legislator asking for an appropriation of $1,500 to erect a monument in the memory of Crispus Attucks, the first martyr in the Boston massacre on the 5th of March 1770. A statue was finely erected in Boston some 37 years later in 1888.

It is written that in the 19th century, Crispus Attucks became the symbol of the abolitionist movement. Crispus Attucks' image and story narrative was seen and told to demonstrate his patriotic virtues. It was then abolitionists like William Cooper Nell and Frederick Douglass extolled Crispus Attucks as the first martyr in the cause of American liberty and used his memory to garner support to end slavery in America and attain equal rights for African Americans.

In the 20th century Attucks' continued to be celebrated as a major African American historical figure. Musician Stevie Wonder wrote a song during the American Revolution Bicentennial that mentioned Crispus Attucks, and a commemorative postage stamp was also issued in his honor. Though little is known of Crispus Attucks' life, his death continues to serve as a reminder that African Americans took an active role in the path to American independence.

Frederick Douglass' position on the Declaration of Independence was given in a speech that was entitled "The Meaning of July Fourth for the Negro":

Fellow Citizens, I am not wanting in respect for the fathers of this republic. The signers of the Declaration of Independence were brave men. They were great men, too (and) great enough to give frame to a great age. It does not often happen to a nation to raise, at one time, such a number of truly great men. The point from which I am compelled to view them is not, certainly, the most favorable; and yet I cannot contemplate their great deeds with less than admiration. They were statesmen, patriots and heroes, and for the good they did, and the principles they contended for, I will unite with you to honor their memory. Fellow-citizens, pardon me, allow me to ask, why am I called upon to speak here today? What have I, or those I represent, to do with your national independence? Are the great principles of political freedom and of natural justice, embodied in that Declaration of Independence, extended to us? And am I, therefore, called upon to bring our humble offering to the national altar and to confess the benefits and express devout gratitude for the blessings resulting from your independence to us? Would to God, both for your sakes and ours, that an affirmative answer could be truthfully returned to these questions! Then would my task be light, and my burden easy and delightful. For who is there so cold, that a nation's sympathy could not warm him? Who so obdurate and dead to the claims of gratitude, that would not thankfully acknowledge such priceless benefits? Who so stolid and selfish, that would not give his voice to swell the hallelujahs of a nation's jubilee, when the chains of servitude had been torn from his limbs? I am not that man. In a case like that, the dumb might eloquently speak, and the lame man leap as a hart. But such is not the state of the case. I say it with a sad sense of the disparity between us. I am not included within the pale of glorious anniversary! Your high independence only reveals the immeasurable distance between us. The blessings in which you, this day, rejoice, are not enjoyed in common. Ñ (In) the rich inheritance of justice, liberty, prosperity and independence, bequeathed by your fathers, is shared by you, not by me. The sunlight that brought light and healing to you, has brought stripes and death to me. This Fourth July is yours, not mine. You may rejoice, I must mourn. To drag a man in fetters into the grand illuminated temple of liberty and call upon him to join you in joyous anthems, were inhuman mockery and sacrilegious irony. Do you mean, citizens, to mock me, by asking me to speak today? If so, there is a parallel to your conduct. And let me warn you that it is dangerous to copy the example of a nation whose crimes, towering up to heaven, were thrown down by the breath of the Almighty, burying that nation in irrevocable ruin! I can today take up the plaintive lament of a peeled and woe-smitten people!

By the rivers of Babylon, there we sat down. Yea! we wept when we remembered Zion. We hanged our harps upon the willows in the midst thereof. For there, they that carried us away captive, required of us a song; and they who wasted us required of us mirth, saying, Sing us one of the songs of Zion. How can we sing the Lord's song in a strange land? If I forget thee, O (Oh} Jerusalem, let my right hand forget her cunning,

And if I do not remember thee then let my tongue cleave to the roof of my mouth. Fellow-citizens, above your national, tumultuous joy, I hear the mournful wail of millions! whose chains, heavy and grievous yesterday, are, to-day, rendered more intolerable by the jubilee shouts that reach them. If I do forget, if I do not faithfully remember those bleeding children of sorrow this day, "may my right hand forget her cunning, and may my tongue cleave to the roof of my mouth!" To forget them, to pass lightly over their wrongs, and to chime in with the popular theme, would be treason most scandalous and shocking, and would make me a reproach before God and the world. My subject, then, fellow-citizens, is American slavery. I shall see this day and its popular characteristics from the slave's point of view. Standing there identified with the American bondman, making his wrongs mine, I do not hesitate to declare, with all my soul, that the character and conduct of this nation never looked blacker to me than on this 4th of July! Whether we turn to the declarations of the past, or to the professions of the present, the conduct of the nation seems equally hideous and revolting. America is false to the past, false to the present, and solemnly binds herself to be false to the future. Standing with God and the crushed and bleeding slave on this occasion, I will, in the name of humanity, which is outraged, in the name of liberty, which is fettered, in the name of the constitution and the Bible which are disregarded and trampled upon, dare to call in question and to denounce, with all the emphasis I can command, everything that serves to perpetuate slavery Ñ (in) the great sin and shame of America! I will not equivocate, I will not excuse", I will use the severest language I can command, and yet not one word shall escape me that any man, whose judgment is not blinded by prejudice, or who is not at heart a slaveholder, shall not confess to be right, and just. But I fancy I hear some one of my audience say, "It is just in this circumstance that you and your brother abolitionists fail to make a favorable impression on the public mind. Would you argue more, and denounce less; would you persuade more, and rebuke less; your cause would be much more likely to succeed." But I submit, where all is plain there is nothing to be argued. What point in the anti-slavery creed would you have me argue? On what branch of the subject do the people of this country need light? Must I undertake to prove that the slave is a man? That point is conceded already. Nobody doubts it. The slaveholders themselves acknowledge it in the enactment of laws for their government. They acknowledge it when they punish disobedience on the part of the slave. There are seventy-two crimes in the State of Virginia, which, if committed by a black man (no matter how ignorant he be), subject him to the punishment of death, while only two of the same crimes will subject a white man to the like punishment. What is this but the acknowledgment that the slave is a moral, intellectual, and responsible being? The manhood of the slave is conceded. It is admitted in the fact that Southern statute books are covered with enactments forbidding, under severe fines and penalties, the teaching of the slave to read or to write.

When you can point to any such laws in reference to the beasts of the field, then I may consent to argue the manhood of the slave. When the dogs in your streets, when the fowls of the air, when the cattle on your hills, when the fish of the sea, and the reptiles that crawl, shall be unable to distinguish the slave from a brute, then will I argue with you that the *slave is a man!*

For the present, it is enough to affirm the equal manhood of the Negro race. Is it not astonishing that, while we are ploughing, planting, and reaping, using all kinds of mechanical tools, erecting houses, constructing bridges, building ships, working in metals of brass, iron, copper, silver and gold; that, while we are reading, writing and ciphering, acting as clerks, merchants and secretaries, having among us lawyers, doctors, ministers, poets, authors, editors, orators and teachers; that, while we are engaged in all manner of enterprises common to other men, digging gold in California, capturing the whale in the Pacific, feeding sheep and cattle on the hillside, living, moving, acting, thinking, planning, living in families as husbands, wives and children, and, above all, confessing and worshipping the Christian's God, and looking hopefully for life and immortality beyond the grave, we are called upon to prove that we are men! Would you have me argue that man is entitled to liberty? That he is the rightful owner of his own body? You have already declared it. Must I argue the wrongfulness of slavery? Is that a question for Republicans? Is it to be settled by the rules of logic and argumentation, as a matter beset with great difficulty, involving a doubtful application of the principle of justice, hard to be understood? How should I look to-day, in the presence of Americans, dividing, and subdividing a discourse, to show that men have a natural right to freedom? speaking of it relatively and positively, negatively, and affirmatively. To do so, would be to make myself ridiculous, and to offer an insult to your understanding.

There is not a man beneath the canopy of heaven that does not know that slavery is wrong for him. What, am I to argue that it is wrong to make men brutes, to rob them of their liberty, to work them without wages, to keep them ignorant of their relations to their fellow men, to beat them with sticks, to flay their flesh with the lash, to load their limbs with irons, to hunt them with dogs, to sell them at auction, to sunder their families, to knock out their teeth, to burn their flesh, to starve them into obedience and submission to their masters? Must I argue that a system thus marked with blood, and stained with pollution, is wrong? No! I will not.

I have better employment for my time and strength than such arguments would imply. What, then, remains to be argued? Is it that slavery is not divine; that God did not establish it; that our Doctor of Divinity are mistaken? There is blasphemy in the thought. That which is inhuman, cannot be divine! Who can reason on such a proposition?

They that can-ma (may), but I cannot, the time for such argument is passed. At a time like this, scorching irony, not convincing argument, is needed. O! (Oh) had I the ability, and could reach the nation's ear, I would, today, pour out a fiery stream of biting ridicule, blasting reproach, withering sarcasm, and stern rebuke. For it is not light that is needed, but fire; it is not the gentle shower, but thunder. We need the storm, the whirlwind, and the earthquake.

The feeling of the nation must be quickened; the conscience of the nation must be roused; the propriety of the nation must be startled; the hypocrisy of the nation must be exposed; and its crimes against God and man must be proclaimed and denounced. What, to the American slave, is your 4th of July? I answer, a day that reveals to him, more than all other days in the year, the gross injustice and cruelty to which he is the constant victim. To him, your celebration is a sham; your boasted liberty, an unholy license; your national greatness, swelling vanity; your sounds of rejoicing are empty and heartless; your denunciation of tyrants, brass fronted impudence; your shouts of liberty and equality, hollow mockery; your prayers and hymns, your sermons and thanksgivings, with all your religious parade and solemnity, are, to Him, mere bombast, fraud, deception, impiety, and hypocrisy, a thin veil to cover up crimes which would disgrace a nation of savages.

There is not a nation on the earth guilty of practices more shocking, and bloodier, than are the people of the United States, at this very hour. Go where you may, search where you will, roam through all the monarchies and despotisms of the Old World, travel through South America, search out every abuse, and when you have found the last, lay your facts by the side of the everyday practices of this nation, and you will say with me, that, for revolting barbarity and shameless hypocrisy, America reigns without a rival.

Allow me to say, in conclusion, notwithstanding the dark picture I have this day presented, of the state of the nation, I do not despair of this country. There are forces in operation which must inevitably work the downfall of slavery. "The arm of the Lord is not shortened," and the doom of slavery is certain.

I, therefore, leave off where I began, with hope. While drawing encouragement from "the Declaration of Independence," the great principles it contains, and the genius of American Institutions, my spirit is also cheered by the obvious tendencies of the age. Nations do not now stand in the same relation to each other that they did ages ago. No nation can now shut itself up from the surrounding world and trot round in the same old path of its fathers without interference. The time was when such could be done. Long established customs of hurtful character could formerly fence themselves in and do their evil work with social impunity. Knowledge was then confined and enjoyed by the privileged few, and the multitude walked on in mental darkness. But a change has now come over the affairs of mankind. Walled cities and empires have become unfashionable. The arm of commerce has borne away the gates of the strong city. Intelligence is penetrating the darkest corners of the globe. It makes its pathway over and under the sea, as well as on the earth. Wind, steam, and lightning are its chartered agents. Oceans no longer divide, but link nations together. From Boston to London is now a holiday excursion. Space is comparatively annihilated.

Thoughts expressed on one side of the Atlantic are distinctly heard on the other. The far off and almost fabulous Pacific rolls in grandeur at our feet. The Celestial Empire, the mystery of ages, is being solved. The fiat of the Almighty, "Let there be Light," has not yet spent its force. No abuse, no outrage whether in taste, sport, or avarice, can now hide itself from the all-pervading light. The iron shoe, and crippled foot of China must be seen in contrast with nature. Africa must rise and put on her yet unwoven garment.

Ethiopia, shall, stretch out her hand unto God. In the fervent aspirations of William Lloyd Garrison, I say, and let every heart join in saying it:

> God speed the year of jubilee
> The wide world over!
> When from their galling chains set free,
> The oppressed shall vilely bend the knee,

And wear the yoke of tyranny
Like brutes no more.
That year will come, and freedom's reign,
To man his plundered rights again
Restore.
God speed the day when human blood
Shall cease to flow!
In every clime be understood,
The claims of human brotherhood,
And each return for evil, good,
Not blow for blow;
That day will come all feuds to end,
And change into a faithful friend
Each foe.
God speed the hour, the glorious hour,
When none on earth
Shall exercise a lordly power,
Nor in a tyrant's presence cower;
But to all manhood's stature tower,
By equal birth!
That hour will come, to each, to all,
And from his Prison-house, to thrall
Go forth.
Until that year, day, hour, arrive,
With head, and heart, and hand I'll strive,
To break the rod, and rend the guy,
The spoiler of his prey deprive.
So witness Heaven!
And never from my chosen post,
Whatever the peril or the cost,
Be driven.
The Life and Writings of Frederick Douglass,

Volume II Philip S. Foner
International Publishers Co., Inc., New York, 1950
Pre-Civil War Decade 1850-1860

During the Reconstruction era, history shows that Frederick Douglas made demands that the government take action to secure land, voting rights, and civil equality for African Americans. The following passage is excerpted from a speech given by Fredrick Douglass to the Massachusetts Anti-Slavery Society in April 1865. Entitled The Reconstruction Era and the Fragility of Democracy.

We may be asked, I say, why we want it [the right to vote]. I will tell you why we want it. We want it because it is our *right*, first of all. No class of men can, without insulting their own nature, be content with any deprivation of their rights. We want it again, as a means for educating our race. Men are so constituted that they derive their conviction of their own possibilities largely from the estimate formed of them by others. If nothing is expected of a people, that people will find it difficult to contradict that expectation. By depriving us of suffrage, you affirm our incapacity to form an intelligent judgment respecting public men and public measures; you declare before the world that we are unfit to exercise the elective franchise, and by this means lead us to undervalue ourselves, to put a low estimate upon ourselves, and to feel that we have no possibilities like other men.

What I ask for the Negro is not benevolence, not pity, not sympathy, but simply *justice*. The American people have always been anxious to know what they shall do with us. Everybody has asked the question, and they learned to ask it early of the abolitionists, "What shall we do with the Negro?" I have had but one answer from the beginning. Do nothing with us!... All I ask is, give him a chance to stand on his own legs! Let him alone! If you see him on his way to school, let him alone, don't disturb him! If you see him going to the dinner-table at a hotel, let him go! If you see him going to the ballot-box, let him alone, don't disturb him!

On January 1, 1863, was the official date for freedom from slavery for African Americans, but African Americans in Texas were unaware about their freedom until June 19, 1865!

CHAPTER FOURTEEN

THE "JUNETEENTH" FREEDOM DAY

The Emancipation Proclamation for freedom Act, that lead to the "Juneteenth Day", to many that have advocated for the legacy of Crispus Attucks, will make a direct linkage in the American history to the historical enactment and sacrifice of Crispus Attucks, who was the 1st to defy, and the 1st to die, for American Independence and Equal Human Rights.

From Wikipedia, the free encyclopedia

Juneteenth (officially Juneteenth National Independence Day and historically known as Jubilee Day, Black Independence Day, and Emancipation Day). It is a federal holiday in the United States commemorating the emancipation of enslaved African Americans. It is also often observed for celebrating African American culture.

Originating in Galveston, Texas, Juneteenth has been celebrated annually on June 19th in various parts of the United States since 1866. The day was recognized as a federal holiday on June 17, 2021, when President Joe Biden signed the Juneteenth National Independence Day Act into law. Juneteenth's commemoration is on the anniversary date of the June 19, 1865, announcement of General Order No. 3 by Union Army General Gordon Granger, proclaiming and enforcing freedom of enslaved people in Texas, which was the last state of the Confederacy with institutional slavery.

President Abraham Lincoln's Emancipation Proclamation of 1862 had officially outlawed slavery in Texas and in all of the other states of the original Confederacy. Enforcement of the Proclamation generally relied upon the advance of Union troops. Texas, as the most remote state of the former Confederacy, had seen an expansion of slavery and had a low presence of Union troops as the American Civil War ended; thus, enforcement there had been slow and inconsistent prior to Granger's announcement.

Although the Emancipation Proclamation declared an end to slavery in the Confederate States, for a short while after the fall of the Confederacy, due to certain political considerations, slavery remained legal in the two Union border states, Delaware and Kentucky. This seemingly conflicted situation ended both with the ratification of the Thirteenth Amendment to the Constitution which constitutionally abolished chattel slavery nationwide on December 6, 1865, and also with the final actual release of slaves in the Indian Territories that had sided with the Confederacy, namely the Choctaw, in 1866.

Celebrations date to 1866, first involving church-centered community gatherings in Texas. It spread across the South and became more commercialized in the 1920s and 1930s, often centering on a food festival. Participants in the Great Migration out of the South carried their celebrations to other parts of the country. During the Civil Rights Movement of the 1960s, these celebrations were eclipsed by the nonviolent determination to achieve civil rights. These grew in popularity again in the 1970s with a focus on African American freedom and African-American arts. Beginning with Texas by proclamation in 1938, and by legislation in 1979, 49 U.S. states and the District of Columbia have formally recognized the holiday in various ways. With its adoption in certain parts of Mexico, the holiday became an international holiday. Juneteenth is celebrated by the "Mascogos", descendants of Black Seminoles who escaped from slavery in 1852 and settled in Coahuila, Mexico.

A group photograph of thirty-one people at a Juneteenth Celebration in Emancipation Park in Houston's Fourth Ward in 1880. PHOTO: Wikimedia Commons

Celebratory traditions often include public readings of the Emancipation Proclamation, singing traditional songs such as "Swing Low, Sweet Chariot", "Lift Every Voice and Sing", and the reading of works by noted African-American writers, such as Ralph Ellison and more recently in the 20th century, Maya Angelou. On June 15, 2021, Juneteenth became a federal holiday with the passage of the Juneteenth National Independence Day Act. Juneteenth is now the first new federal holiday since Martin Luther King Jr. Day was declared a holiday in 1983.

The Civil War and the celebrations of emancipation by freed slaves.

During the American Civil War (1861–1865), emancipation came at different times to various places. In the Southern United States, large celebrations of emancipation often called Jubilees (recalling biblical stories in which slaves were freed) occurred on various dates ie. September 22, January 1, July 4, August 1, April 6, and November 1, among others.

In Texas, emancipation came alarmingly late: until enforced on June 19, 1865, as the southern rebellion collapsed, emancipation became a well-known cause for celebration. While June 19, 1865, did not totally end Chattel slavery, even in Texas, General Gordon's military order had to be acted upon while competing with other dates for emancipation. Ordinary African Americans created, preserved, and spread a shared commemoration of slavery's wartime demise across the United States, hence "Juneteenth".

The "Juneteenth" Freedom Day

Major General Gordon Granger

Major General Gordon Granger issued General Order No. 3 formally informing Texas residents that slavery had ended.

President Abraham Lincoln issued the Emancipation Proclamation on September 22, 1862 It became effective on January 1, 1863, declaring that all enslaved persons in the Confederate States of America in rebellion and not in Union hands were freed.

More isolated geographically, planters and other slaveholders had migrated into Texas from eastern states to escape the fighting. Many brought enslaved people with them, increasing by the thousands the enslaved population in the state by the end of the war. Although most lived in rural areas, several thousand resided in both Galveston, and Houston. By 1860, thousands more had migrated in other large towns. By 1865, there were an estimated 250,000 enslaved people in Texas.

Despite the surrender of General Robert E. Lee at Appomattox Court House on April 9, 1865, the western Army of the Trans-Mississippi did not surrender until June 2. On the morning of June 19, 1865. Union Major General Gordon Granger arrived on the island of Galveston, Texas, to take command of the more than 2,000 federal troops that recently landed in the state of Texas to enforce the freeing of its slaves and to oversee the peaceful transition of power. The mission for Granger and his soldiers was to make null and void all laws passed within Texas by Confederate lawmakers. The Texas Historical Commission and Galveston Historical Foundation report that Granger's men marched throughout Galveston reading General Order No. 3, first at Union Army Headquarters, at the Osterman Building formerly at the intersection of Strand Street and 22nd Street, since demolished (in the Strand Historic District).

They then marched to the Customs House and Courthouse before finally marching to the Negro Church on Broadway, which has since been renamed Reedy Chapel-AME Church. The order informed all Texans that, in accordance with the Proclamation from the Executive Office of the United States, all slaves were free:

The people of Texas are informed that, in accordance, by proclamation by the President of the United States, all slaves are free. This involves an absolute equality of personal rights and rights of property between former masters and slaves, and the connection heretofore existing between them becomes that between employer and hired labor. The freedmen are advised to remain quietly in their present homes and work for wages. They are informed that they will not be allowed to collect at military posts and that they will not be supported in idleness either there or elsewhere.

Longstanding urban legend places the historic reading of General Order No. 3 at Ashton Villa; however, no extant historical evidence supports such claims. On June 21, 2014, the Galveston Historical Foundation and Texas Historical Commission erected a Juneteenth plaque where the Osterman Building once stood signifying the location of Major General Granger's Union Headquarters and subsequent issuance of his general orders.

Although this event has come to be celebrated as the end of slavery, emancipation for the remaining enslaved in two Union border states (Delaware and Kentucky), would not come until several months later on December 18, 1865, when the ratification of the Thirteenth Amendment, was finally announced. The freedom of formerly enslaved people in Texas was given state law status in a series of Texas Supreme Court decisions between 1868 and 1874.

Formerly enslaved people in Galveston celebrated after the announcement. On June 19, 1866, one year after the announcement, freedmen in Texas organized the first of what became the annual celebration of "Jubilee Day". Early celebrations were used as political rallies to give voting instructions to newly freed African Americans. Early independence celebrations often occurred on January 1 or 4.

It is important to know that In some cities, black people were barred from using public parks because of state-sponsored segregation of facilities. Across parts of Texas, freed people pooled their funds to purchase land to hold their own celebrations. The day was first celebrated in Austin in 1867 under the auspices of the Freedmen's Bureau, and it had been listed on a "calendar of public events" by 1872. That year, black leaders in Texas raised $1,000 for the purchase of 10 acres of land to celebrate Juneteenth, today known as Houston's Emancipation Park. The observation was soon drawing thousands of attendees across Texas; an estimated 30,000 black people celebrated at Booker T. Washington Park in Limestone County, Texas, established in 1898 for Juneteenth celebrations. By the 1890s, Jubilee Day had become known as Juneteenth.

Celebration of Emancipation Day (Juneteenth) in 1900, Texas

Emancipation Day celebration in Richmond, Virginia, 1905

In the early 20th century, economic and political forces led to a decline in Juneteenth celebrations. From 1890 to 1908, Texas and all former Confederate states passed new constitutions or amendments that effectively disenfranchised black people, excluding them from the political process. White-dominated state legislatures passed Jim Crow laws imposing second-class status. Gladys L. Knight writes the decline in celebrations occurred because "upwardly mobile blacks, were ashamed of their slave past and aspired to assimilate into mainstream culture. Younger generations of blacks, became further removed from the history of slavery and were occupied with school and other pursuits." Others who migrated to the Northern States could not take time off or they simply ignored or forgot the celebration.

The Great Depression forced many black people off farms and into the cities to find work, where they had difficulty taking the day off to celebrate. From 1936 to 1951, the Texas State Fair served as a destination for celebrating the holiday, contributing to its revival. In

1936, an estimated 150,000 to 200,000 people joined the holiday's celebration in Dallas. In 1938, the Governor of Texas, James V. Allred issued a proclamation stating in part:

Whereas the Negroes in the State of Texas observe June 19 as the official day for the celebration of Emancipation from slavery and

Whereas, June 19, 1865, was the date when General Robert S. Granger, who had command of the Military District of Texas, issued a proclamation notifying the Negroes of Texas that they were free; and

Whereas, since that time, Texas Negroes have observed this day with suitable holiday ceremony, except during such years when the day comes on a Sunday; when the Governor of the State is asked to proclaim the following day as the holiday for State observance by Negroes; and

Whereas, June 19, 1938, this year falls on Sunday; NOW, THEREFORE, I, JAMES V. ALLRED, Governor of the State of Texas, do set aside and proclaim the day of June 20, 1938, as the date for observance of EMANCIPATION DAY

And in Texas do urge all members of the Negro race in Texas to observe the day in a manner appropriate to its importance to them. Seventy thousand people attended a "Juneteenth Jamboree."

In 1951. From 1940 through 1970, in the second wave of the Great Migration, more than five million black people left Texas, Louisiana and other parts of the South for the North and the West Coast. As historian Isabel Wilkerson writes, "The people from Texas took Juneteenth Day to Los Angeles, Oakland, Seattle, and other places they went." In 1945, Juneteenth was introduced in San Francisco by an immigrant from Texas, Wesley Johnson.

During the 1950s and 1960s, the Civil Rights Movement focused the attention of African Americans on expanding freedom and integrating. As a result, observations of the holiday declined again (though it was still celebrated in Texas).

In 1996, the first legislation to recognize "Juneteenth Independence Day" was introduced in the U.S. House of Representatives, H.J. Res. 195, sponsored by Barbara-Rose Collins (D-MI). In 1997, Congress recognized the day through Senate Joint Resolution 11 and House Joint Resolution 56. In 2013, the U.S. Senate passed Senate Resolution 175, acknowledging Lula Briggs Galloway (late president of the National Association of Juneteenth Lineage), who "successfully worked to bring national recognition to Juneteenth Independence Day", and the continued leadership of the National Juneteenth Observance Foundation.

Governor Tom Wolf signing legislation to officially recognize Juneteenth in Pennsylvania

In June 2019, Governor of Pennsylvania Tom Wolf recognized Juneteenth as a holiday in the state. 2020, state governors of Virginia, New York, and New Jersey signed an executive order recognizing Juneteenth as a paid day of leave for state employees. In 2021, Governor of Oregon Kate Brown signed an executive order recognizing Juneteenth as a paid day of leave for state employees. On June 16, 2021, Illinois Governor J. B. Pritzker signed House Bill 3922, establishing Juneteenth as a paid state holiday starting in ceremonial observance in Illinois. 2022; since 2003, it had been a state.

Activists had long been pushing Congress to recognize Juneteenth. Organizations such as the National Juneteenth Observance Foundation sought a Congressional designation of Juneteenth as a national day of observance. When it was officially made a federal holiday on June 17, 2021, it became one of five date-specific federal holidays along with New Year's Day (January 1), Independence Day (July 4), Veterans Day (November 11), and Christmas Day (December 25). Juneteenth will coincide with Father's Day in 2022, 2033, 2039, 2044, and 2050. Juneteenth is the first new federal holiday since Martin Luther King Jr. Day was declared a holiday in 1986.

Since the 1980s and 1990s, the holiday has been more widely celebrated among African American communities and has seen increasing mainstream attention in the US. In 1991, there was an exhibition by the Anacostia Museum (part of the Smithsonian Institution) called "Juneteenth '91, Freedom Revisited". In 1994, a group of community leaders gathered at Christian Unity Baptist Church in New Orleans to work for greater national celebration of Juneteenth. Expatriates have celebrated it in cities abroad, such as Paris. Some US military bases in other countries sponsor celebrations, in addition to those of private groups. In 1999, Ralph Ellison's novel *Juneteenth* was published, increasing recognition of the holiday. By 2006, at least 200 cities celebrated the day.

The "Juneteenth" Freedom Day

Created in 1997 by: Ben Haith the Juneteenth Flag

In 1997, activist Ben Haith created the Juneteenth flag, which was further refined by illustrator Lisa Jeanne Graf. In 2000, the flag was first hoisted at the Roxbury Heritage State Park in Boston by Haith. The star at the center represents Texas and the extension of freedom for all African Americans throughout the whole nation. The burst around the star represents a nova and the curve represents a horizon, standing for a new era for African Americans. The red, white, and blue colors represent the American flag, which shows that African Americans and their enslaved ancestors are Americans, and the national belief in liberty and justice for all citizens. The Pan-African flag is also displayed during the holiday.

The 21st Century Commemoration and History of Crispus Attucks Day

Designed by: Marcus Garvey the Pan-African Flag

The Juneteenth Holiday has gained mainstream awareness outside African-American communities through depictions in entertainment media, such as episodes from the TV series *Atlanta* in (2016) and *Blackish* (2017), the latter of which featured musical numbers about the holiday by music artist Aloe Blacc, The Roots, and Fonzworth Bentley.

In 2018, Apple computers apps added Juneteenth to its calendars in **iOS** under official U.S. holidays. Some private companies have adopted Juneteenth as a paid day off for employees, while others have officially marked the day in other ways, such as moments of silence. In 2020, several American corporations and educational institutions, including Twitter, the National Football League, and Nike, announced that they would treat Juneteenth as a company holiday, providing a paid day off to their workers, and Google Calendar added Juneteenth to its U.S. Holidays calendar.

Also in 2020, several major universities formally recognized Juneteenth, either as a "day of reflection" or as a university holiday with paid time off for faculty and staff.

2003. Congresswoman Sheila Jackson Lee campaigned for Juneteenth to be a federal holiday

Juneteenth is now a National federal holiday in the United States. For decades, activists and congress members (led by many African American activists) proposed legislation, advocated for, and built support for state and national observances. During his successful campaign for president in June 2020, Joe Biden publicly celebrated the holiday. Spurred on by the advocates and the Congressional Black Caucus, on June 15, 2021, the Senate unanimously passed the Juneteenth National Independence Day Act, establishing Juneteenth as a federal holiday.

It subsequently passed through the House of Representatives by a vote of 415 yes and 14 no, on June 16. President Joe Biden signed the bill on June 17, 2021, making Juneteenth the eleventh American federal holiday and the first to obtain legal observance as a federal holiday since Martin Luther King Jr. Day was designated in 1983.

The holiday is considered the "longest-running African-American holiday "and has been called "America's second Independence Day". Juneteenth is usually celebrated on the third Saturday in June. Historian Mitch Kachun considers that celebrations of the end of slavery have three goals: "to celebrate, to educate, and to agitate". Early celebrations consisted of baseball, fishing, and rodeos. African Americans were often prohibited from using public facilities for their celebrations, so they were often held at churches or near water. Celebrations were also characterized by elaborate large meals and people wearing their best clothing. It was common for former slaves and their descendants to make a pilgrimage to Galveston. As early festivals received news coverage, Janice Hume and Noah Arceneaux consider that they "served to assimilate African-American memories within the dominant 'American story'. "

Observance today is primarily in local celebrations. In many places, Juneteenth has become a multicultural holiday. Celebrations include picnics, rodeos, street fairs, cookouts, family reunions, park parties, historical reenactments, blues festivals and Miss Juneteenth contests. Strawberry soda is a traditional drink associated with the celebration. The Mascogos, the descendants of Black Seminoles, who have resided in Coahuila, Mexico, since 1852, also celebrate Juneteenth.

Juneteenth celebrations often include lectures and exhibitions on African American culture. The modern holiday places much emphasis upon teaching about African American heritage. Karen M. Thomas wrote in *Emerge* that "community leaders have latched on to [Juneteenth] to help instill a sense of heritage and pride in black youth." Celebrations are commonly accompanied by voter registration efforts, the performing of plays, and retelling stories. The holiday is also a celebration of soul food and other food with African American influences.

In *Tourism Review International*, Anne Donovan and Karen DeBres write that "Barbecue is the centerpiece of most Juneteenth celebrations".

CHAPTER FIFTEEN
SUSAN B. ANTHONY

1852: Susan B. Anthony, was from a Quaker family with long activist traditions. Early in her life she developed a sense of justice and moral zeal. She was born in Massachusetts and as a teacher, she was aware of Crispus Attucks as being the Boston martyr for human rights, as also being synonymous for women's rights. She became active in what was called the temperance movement at that time, but because she was a woman, she was not allowed to speak and that led her to join the women's rights movement. Soon after, she dedicated her life to the woman's suffrage cause.

CHAPTER SIXTEEN

WILLIAM COOPER NELL

1858: William Cooper Nell established "Crispus Attucks Day!" in Boston, honoring the only African American among the five men killed in the Boston Massacre nearly a century earlier. Nell was outraged by the US Supreme Court ruling in *Dred Scott v. Sandford* ruling in 1857, which outraged most African American Abolitionists and activists. He said that ethnic Africans had no legal standing in the United States as they were not considered as citizens, under the Constitution.

Nell organized a memorial celebration for Crispus Attucks at Faneuil Hall, which was a traditional site of Attucks commemoration, and worked with others to have a "Crispus Attucks Day" designated in Boston. He reminded people of the participation of African Americans in the fight for independence from Great Britain and helped have Attucks recognized in the commemoration of the Boston Massacre. That same year, Nell organized the Convention of Colored Citizens of New England. While it was contrary to his earlier dislike of segregated abolitionist efforts, he argued that the Dred *Scott* decision was such an insult to blacks that they needed to act separately, and in a meaningful way.

Nell served as publisher for Frederick Douglass' *The North Star*, from late 1847 until 1851, moving temporarily to Rochester, New York, during this period. He also joined New York anti-slavery societies and founded a literary society. William Cooper Nell was a tireless advocate of racial integration, in the military and social institutions, as well as in schools. He critiqued not only segregationist practices instituted by whites, but also the separatist churches and voluntary organizations formed by blacks, and it is important to note that Nell's own father, William Guion Nell, had belonged to one.

Most of his life in Boston, William Cooper Nell was a member of the then abolitionist circle surrounding William Lloyd Garrison and he worked for Garrison's antislavery newspaper, the *Liberator*. In addition to abolitionism, Nell advocated a range of beliefs and reforms that were popular in the mid-nineteenth century, including women's rights, temperance, and spiritualism. Perhaps Nell's most valuable weapon in his antislavery arsenal was his knowledge of history. Although he frequently wrote articles for the *Liberator* and other activist newspapers, Nell's most important work as an artist or writer was *The Colored Patriots of the American Revolution* (1855). It was a product of Nell's painstaking research in government archives, newspapers, and graveyards and his interviews with survivors of the Revolutionary War and their descendants. This accumulation gathered every available scrap of information about the African American involvement as the patriot side of the Revolution. The immediate motivation for this research was the Massachusetts legislature's refusal to erect a monument for Crispus Attucks, the runaway slave shot by the British military guards, in the Boston Massacre on March 5, 1770.

Today, Attucks is widely regarded as the first American casualty of the Revolution; in the mid-nineteenth century. Before Nell's publications, Crispus Attucks had been all but forgotten. Nell's goal in recovering the memory of Attucks and other men and women of color who had supported the American Revolution was to ignite a righteous fire to the abolitionist movement.

CHAPTER SEVENTEEN
WILLIAM MONROE TROTTER

William Monroe Trotter, sometimes just Monroe Trotter, was a newspaper editor and real estate businessman based in Boston, Massachusetts, and an activist African American leader for civil rights.

William Monroe Trotter was a graduate of Harvard University along with W.E.B. DuBois. They were contemporaries at Harvard and briefly worked together as leaders of a group of African American intellectuals known as the Niagara Movement. But Trotter withdrew from the movement to form the National Equal Rights League and later refused to join the newly-formed National Association for the Advancement of Colored People because of his distrust of the white leadership.

At that time, Trotter's style of advocacy did not favor him to other African American leaders, and because of his single mindedness tendency and inability to compromise with others, he was labelled as fanaticism by some of his critics. In 1912 Trotter endorsed Democrat Woodrow Wilson for the presidency, but the new president was seen as disrespecting Trotter by repaying his African American support by segregating African American workers in the federal government.

Trotter then led a delegation of African Americans to the White House and for 45 minutes he and Wilson stood toe to toe and debated the president's action. Wilson lost his temper, offended by Trotter's "manner" and "tone, with its background of passion," and banned Trotter from the White House for the rest of his term.

In 1922, 1923, 1924 and 1926 William Monroe Trotter led delegations of African Americans to the White House to protest continued segregation in the federal government. He also led demonstrations and pickets against the racist KKK Birth of a Nation, he defended the Scottsboro Boys, and crusaded for a Crispus Attucks Day to honor the African American hero and Revolutionary War Patriot.

CHAPTER EIGHTEEN
JOSEPHINE ST. PIERRE RUFFIN

1869: Josephine St. Pierre Ruffin, born in Boston, was the first African American to graduate from Harvard Law School and later served on the Boston City Council, the state legislature, and became the first black municipal judge in Boston.

In 1910, Josephine helped form the National Association for the Advancement of Colored People (NAACP), a league dedicated to Equal Human Rights. Josephine St. Pierre Ruffin was aware of Attucks' legacy for equal human rights in Boston and America, and she then became motivated to activate for those rights as a woman.

Her activism for social and political multicultural diversity, in leadership, was well known by her and among her constituents in Boston in support of the advocacy of Crispus Attucks, for which he was considered as "The 1st to defy & the 1st to Die" for American liberty.

CHAPTER NINETEEN
CARTER G. WOODSON

1922: Carter G. Woodson – published "The Negro in Our History."

The 21st Century Commemoration and History of Crispus Attucks Day

He stated that Negroes must know the history of the Negro race in America, otherwise they will not get in white institutions. Their children ought to study textbooks like Brawley's "Short History," the first edition of Woodson's "Negro in Our History," and Cromwell, Turner, and Dykes' "Readings from Negro Authors." Negroes, who celebrate the birthdays of Washington and Lincoln, and relatively unimportant "founders" of various Negro colleges, ought not to forget the 5th of March, —that first national holiday of this country, which commemorates the martyrdom of Crispus Attucks.

Carter Woodson was one of the 1[sts] African American graduates from Harvard University with a Dr. degree, and he said in his famous book," The Mis-Education of The Negro", that he had mixed feelings about the classification and surtitle of a Doctors Degree status for a higher Negro learning status. He said that when you think about it, all of this mental excitement that this caused among African Americans' brightest minds in those days just to get a job or training when education is supposed to prepare you to help yourself and others, while training prepares you to do a job.

Too often the so-called Negro forgets why they were brought to America; it was to work and do a job willingly or unwillingly. That was all we as a people were brought here to do. Not govern for themselves and or to be equal with white Americans, which was never in the plans of the original planners or framers in America.

Like General Electric, Ford Motors, Sears and Roebuck, the so-called Negro was a product made in America to make others comfortable or rich from their skills and good labor.

CHAPTER TWENTY
MARTIN LUTHER KING JR

1964: Martin Luther King Jr. was a Graduate of Boston University. In one of his many empowering speeches about Attucks he said, "His name gained even more prominence during the Civil War when abolitionists cited him as the symbol of equality." Martin Luther King Jr. also cited him in his 1964 speech, "Why We Can't Wait," as a man who can be respected for his contribution to history.

He said while many overlook Attucks' contribution to American history, he still provides a powerful example of moral courage that we all should follow. A monument for the Boston Massacre (also known as the Crispus Attucks monument) commemorating the Boston Massacre was erected at the Boston Common in 1888, more than 100 years after the massacre.

Dr. King has further described him as one of the most important figures in African American history "not just what he did for his own race, but for what he did for all oppressed people everywhere. He is a reminder that the African American heritage is not only African but American, and it is a heritage that begins with the beginning of America.

CHAPTER TWENTY-ONE
SENATOR ED BROOKS

1976: Senator Ed. Brooks. On October 17, of that year, he addressed an audience at Faneuil Hall for Crispus Attucks Day, he rightly observed: "Here and now in this room, you and I are still fighting for freedom more than 200 years later."

Brooke condemned the "separate but equal clause in American law"; he affirmed Attucks' reputation as a martyr who "gave his life" for freedom. Boston.1966, Senator Ed. Brooks became the first African American popularly elected to the United States Senate. He represented Massachusetts in the Senate from 1967 to 1979.

CHAPTER TWENTY-TWO
MELNEA AGNES CASS

The 21st Century Commemoration and History of Crispus Attucks Day

1976: Melnea Agnes Cass was an American community and civil rights activist. She helped found the Boston local Brotherhood of Sleeping Car Porters. Cass also assisted women with voter registration after the passage of the Nineteenth Amendment. She was affectionately known as the "First Lady of Roxbury". Before her death in 1976 she helped the Boston Equal Rights League in their activism to present to the city of Boston the Crispus Attucks Commemorative Plaque.

Melnea Cass on March 4, 1970 is speaking at a "Crispus Attucks Day" rally at the site where Crispus Attucks was shot & killed, behind the Old State House.

In the 1920s Melnea Cass, at an incredibly young age, became a member of the National Equal Rights League and she was under the leadership of the great African American abolitionist William Monroe Trotter. Eventually she became the president of the NERL and throughout the 60s and 70s they advocated for fair housing, equal employment and against school segregation. In 1970 Melnea Cass organized activists in Boston, outside of the Old State House on Attucks Day during in collaboration with the 200th anniversary of the Boston Massacre in March 1970. It was at a time of tense conflict in the city, during a time of school desegregation in the city of Boston, after the Brown vs. Board of Education ruling, and Boston did not integrate its schools. African American parents then turned to the National Association for Colored People and the National Equal Rights League for their assistance in the racial discrimination. They then drafted legislation to get the state to investigate racial imbalance in schools. A commission was established and suggested redistricting, but the Boston School Board refused to discuss the proposal.

In response, the State of Massachusetts passed the Racial Imbalance Act in 1965, that then ordered schools to integrate. That led to the NAACP filing a lawsuit against the Boston School Committee. That action set off a nine-year court case that eventually result in very violent conflicts in the streets of Boston, throughout the 60s and 70s. In 1976, as America was celebrating America's bicentennial (200), in the city of Boston, racial tension and the anti-busing riots worsened, Melnea Cass collaborated with other activists and used Crispus Attucks Day on March 5, 1976, to continue their protest of public-school segregation as well as employment discrimination, while then facing violence from white citizens. On May 22, Boston celebrates Melnea Cass Day.

CHAPTER TWENTY-THREE
MALCOM X

Malcom X

1965: Malcom X. Book Opening: (chapter #3) "As Malcolm explored Boston" he stated: Soon I ranged out of Roxbury and began to explore Boston proper. Historic buildings were everywhere I turned, and plaques and markers and statues for famous events and men.

One statue in the Boston Commons astonished me. It was a statue with the inscription: A Negro named Crispus Attucks, who had been the first man to fall in the Boston Massacre. I had never known anything like that. (p. 43). History shows us that Malcom learning about Crispus Attucks, would have a profound effect on his personal ambitions, and his future activism for Civil and Human Rights.

CHAPTER TWENTY-FOUR
SOUTH AFRICA PRESIDENT, NELSON MANDELA

1999: **Nelson Mandela was the 1st Black President of the Republic of South Africa, that made his 1st trip to Boston.** He himself a former freedom fighter and activist was aware of the similar activism he had experienced in South Africa, with Boston's history and legends, like the Boston revolutionary war Patriot, Crispus Attucks.

He said he was honored to be in the birthplace of the American Revolution. On that historical day, more than a quarter of a million people, turned out to cheer the black liberation leader and then Senator Edward M. Kennedy (D-Mass).

Mandela was aware of him standing within a few miles of the sites of the first battle of the Revolutionary War, the Boston Massacre that took place on King Street. Mandela recalled Boston's role in the American independence movement and praised Crispus Attucks, a black man who was the first person killed in that war.

Mandela also praised Massachusetts for being the first state to institute sanctions, in 1977, against South Africa, calling it "the conscience of American society. Mandela said," Together, we have turned the wheel of history in favor of liberty. When one day our history is rewritten, the pioneering role of Massachusetts will stand out like a shining diamond."

CHAPTER TWENTY-FIVE
PRESIDENT BARACK OBAMA

March 5, 2022: the city of Boston will commemorate the 252nd year of the "Boston Massacre" and Crispus Attucks

Commemoration Day. It was on that day Crispus Attucks became known at the beginning of the American Revolutionary war for freedom and equal human rights. In the city of Boston, there are two examples of what now has become known as the roots of multicultural, global, diversity in leadership.

It goes without question that president Obama's tenure as a student was at Harvard University and that he was an African American with a direct lineage to Africa, through his father, who was also a student at Harvard.

Obama had a special sense of pride in knowing the history of Crispus Attucks and that he shared a simular scenario with his own father that also came to Boston from Africa. Obama was aware of Crispus Attucks' history when he was in Boston. He felt inspired and was motivated to become a constitutional lawyer, and became a social leader as a law student at Harard University.

Those simular experiences have been quoted by those who knew him then, and that, metaphorically speaking, the beginning of the historical election of Barack Obama's becoming the first African American President, began on March 5, 1770 at the site of the Boston Massacre, with the courageous enactment of Crispus Attucks.

To many, this factor speaks to the unique timeline in the history of the 21st century new millennium error, in kowing that we the people of Boston will celebrate multicultural-social-academic leadership, with the example, and in the spirit of Crispus Attucks of Multi-cultural gobal- leadership, for equal human rights!

The 21st Century Commemoration and History of Crispus Attucks Day

A MESSAGE TO AMERICA FROM THE AFRICAN DIASPORA IN THE 21ST CENTURY!

Left to right The FOCAA Department on African Advisory Affairs: Director, Abdou Thiaw, and FOCAA President: Haroon Rashid. PHOTO by Wayne Ysaguirre

"One of the most damaging aspects of the Transatlantic Slave trade was the success the Europeans had in pinning Africans against Africans, thus allowing them to succeed in rampaging to their benefit the African continent for over four hundred years. In doing so they deprived it of a massive human capital they used to move forward their economies and societies while depriving the Black continent of its natural resources.

As an African-born American citizen, I have not a single doubt in my mind that the sin of slavery deserves financial reparation. While I have great pain in reminding myself that some of the slaves were uprooted from the Motherland by African actors turned slave suppliers, I can't help but think that the African continent as a whole, was victimized by the evil actions of bigger military powers of that time.

There lies my motivation, to re-establish the link with our American brothers. We are in this together. For centuries we have been told we were sub-humans because of the color of our skin.

From 366 years of slavery to the Jim Crow, Apartheid, and Colonization, we have suffered the lack of proper acknowledgment of centuries when great Black Empires had flourished and dominated, going all the way back to the ancient civilization of the Nile Valley in Egypt and the Meroe Empire, to the Mali Empire, with Timbuktu as its capital to name a few. Now is the time to correct some of these wrongs, and the acknowledgment of Crispus Attucks as an African American Hero of its own is just one little step in that direction."

- **Abdou Thiaw**

The 21st Century Commemoration and History of Crispus Attucks Day

The FOCAA Board Members: at the site of The Old State House historic building in Boston, Massachusetts. Built in 1713, from left to right: Azell Martin, Robert Redd, Cynthia Strong, James Harris, Nathaniel Smith, Kelly Smith, Rickie Thompson and Haroon Rashid: PHOTO by, Wayne Ysaguirre

This is where beginning of the Boston Massacre took place at The Old State House, and it is a historic building in Boston, Massachusetts. Built in 1713, it was the seat of the *Massachusett*s General Court until 1798. It is located at the intersection of Washington and State Streets and is one of the oldest public buildings in the United States.

One of the landmarks on Boston's Freedom Trail, it is the oldest surviving public building in Boston, and now serves as a history museum that, through 2019, was operated by the Bostonian Society until January 2020. On January 1, 2020, the Bostonian Society merged with the Old South Association in Boston to form Revolutionary

Spaces. The Old State House was designated a National Historic Landmark in 1960 and a Boston Landmark by the Boston Landmarks Commission in 1994.

On March 5, 1770, the Boston Massacre occurred in front of the building on Devonshire Street. Lieutenant Governor Thomas Hutchinson stood on the building's balcony to speak to the people, ordering the crowd to return to their homes.

ABOUT THE AUTHORS

The FOCAA Board Members: at the 1886, Boston Massacre Marker-Pavement Medallion, that marks the site of the Boston Massacre: from left to right, Azell Martin, Robert Redd, Cynthia Strong, James Harris, Kelly Smith, Nathaniel Smith, Haroon Rashid and Rickie Thompson: PHOTO by, Wayne Ysaguirre

In 2019 The Friends of Crispus Attucks Association (FOCAA) was founded by a group of Boston social community activists who collectively saw the need for a new and more humane way of commemorating Crispus Attucks' legacy in the 21st century, as one that will give more dignity to his life and ultimately his death than what has been publicly given in the past.

About the Authors

It was then that Haroon A. Rashid, James Harris, Robert Redd, Cynthia Strong, Ricky Thompson, Nathaniel Smith, Kelly Smith, Azell Martin Abdou Thiaw, Paul Goodnight, and Joe Pendarvis organized and then registered the FOCAA as a Not-for-Profit social-political corporation in The City of Boston that represents the legacy of America's first Revolutionary War Patriot, and the Boston Massacre Hero: Crispus Attucks.

We were aware that there are and have been many American scholars and historians that will tell you what has happened on March 5th in 1770 that made Attucks into a Boston Martyr. However, little or no one has publicly declared the most valuable need to know information about his historical enactment, and that is "Why" The Friends of Crispus Attucks Association NFP, mission in the city of Boston and the state of Massachusetts is to answer that question and to preserve "The Spirit of Attucks" legacy, as it relates in the 21st century to multicultural global diversity in leadership and inclusion for "Human Rights".

In doing this, the Friends of Crispus Attucks has created a form of outreach to the public and private leaderships locally, nationally, and internationally to partner for this new dignified narrative of the Boston Martyr.

One of the Friends of Crispus Attucks' goals is to proudly motivate and encourage Boston youths in leadership awareness, "In the Spirit of Crispus Attucks", which is to analyze and advocate for 21st-century human rights in The City of Boston and The State of Massachusetts.

We thank you, for reading our publication.

www.ingramcontent.com/pod-product-compliance
Lightning Source LLC
Chambersburg PA
CBHW070610010526
44118CB00012B/1479